Together
FOREVER

Together FOREVER

Gospel Perspectives for Marriage and Family

DOUGLAS E. BRINLEY

Bookcraft
Salt Lake City, Utah

Library of Congress Catalog Card Number 98-73234
ISBN 1-57008-540-4

First Printing, 1998

Printed in the United States of America

To Geri, my eternal companion

Contents

Acknowledgments

My thanks to Bookcraft for their encouragement and help in articulating this message. Special thanks go to both George Bickerstaff for making this readable, and to Cory Maxwell for his assistance in seeing it through to completion.

I have a special appreciation for the folks at Bookcraft, who not only have been good friends but also have encouraged me in my efforts to discuss marriage and family topics over the years.

Introduction

On the night of the angel Moroni's first visit to the Prophet Joseph Smith he announced "that the preparatory work for the second coming of the Messiah was speedily to commence; that the time was at hand for the Gospel in all its fullness to be preached in power, unto all nations, that a people might be prepared for the Millennial reign." (Joseph Smith, History of the Church [*HC*] 4:537.)

As Latter-day Saints we are responsible for and deeply involved in that preparatory work that is "speedily" moving forward. We are called upon to perform the overwhelming task of preparing the earth for the second coming of Jesus Christ. This effort requires us to take the gospel to the earth's inhabitants, establish a righteous people before the Savior returns, and build temples for ordinance work in behalf both of the living and of those who have passed into the spirit world. When we consider the profound nature of our stewardship we realize that success will require our very best efforts as individuals, couples, and families. To establish Zion is a feat of immense magnitude, as witnessed by the fact that it has been accomplished only twice in any sizeable numbers in the world's history: The city of Enoch, and the Nephites for two centuries following the resurrected Lord's visit.[1]

This goal is prodigious from a logistical standpoint too. Our assignment to cover the entire globe with the message of the Restoration is a task that will require tens of thousands of missionaries. Yet Latter-day Saints represent only two percent of the American population. Perhaps just as challenging though more subtle is the fact that we are to build Zion while we are blessed with unparalleled prosperity. Scriptural precedents show that whenever the house of Israel was blessed temporally they tossed aside their faith and began, instead, to imitate, absorb, and adopt the lifestyle of those they were sent to save. That mistake must not happen again.

Of course we need a standard of living sufficient to allow families funds to send their sons and daughters on missions to the four quarters of the earth, and the Church depends on tithing from the Saints to build chapels and temples around the world. We are blessed to have airplanes, computers, automobiles, printing presses, and the ability to keep in touch with the Saints throughout the world by satellite. (I often wonder what the Apostle Paul could have done with a helicopter, microwaves, reception dishes, fax machines, telephones, interstate highways, automobiles, and e-mail.) The Lord has inspired an amazing array of technology to preach the gospel and gather Israel. From these inventions, however, has come an increased level of income for many, with the probability of spiritual complacency a real danger. Nephi called it the "all-is-well-in-Zion" syndrome of our day. But this time we must have a different outcome than did God's former people in America: the people of Noah, the Jaredites, the Nephites, or even our own members in the formative days of Kirtland, Missouri, and Illinois. We are learning how difficult it is to build a people of faith in an era of prosperity.

OUR HOMES: THE STARTING PLACE

Our homes are the seedbeds from which this effort is to bloom and blossom. Prophets have clearly and repeatedly taught that the greatest work in this period of history will succeed or fail according to how well we function at home as husbands and wives, fathers and mothers. We know now that weak marriages produce weak individuals, who produce weak and broken families. If that pattern were to persist, the message of the Restoration would be in grave danger, for who else could or would be interested in extending the kingdom of God? Who else could expand the work begun by God's call of a latter-day prophet? There is no other people to do it.[2] Our charge is to change the spiritual direction of the Father's family. We are called to be the salt of the earth.[3] We must preserve family values in a world of shifting moral standards, a society mired in a do-your-own-thing ethics.

Latter-day Saints must demonstrate to the world that the restoration of gospel principles in our day is an advantage over the present forms of religion. We must show others that one of the most visible products of this work is the impact that the gospel has on marriage and family life. Here is the pattern we want to duplicate: *Stable individuals produce stable marriages, and they in turn produce stable families who produce stable individuals.* Quality home life is our best magnet to attract others to the gospel plan. President Spencer W. Kimball said, "Our success . . . as a church will largely be determined by how faithfully we focus on living the gospel in the home" (*Ensign,* May 1979, p. 83). President Gordon B. Hinckley pleaded: "Let us work together, every one of us, to build the kingdom, to tell our neighbors, to help the missionaries, to live the kind of lives which will cause other people to ask about us. That will be the greatest thing that we can do." (At Quito, Ecuador, August 12, 1997; *Church News,* February 7, 1998, p. 2.)

Church media commit us to set the example in family living. A proclamation on the family went out in 1995, under the united voice of prophets, seers, and revelators, telling the world that Latter-day Saints are serious about family life. When Church members experience failure in family living (divorce, physical and sexual abuse, premarital pregnancies, other sexual immorality, rebellious children, broken covenants), not only do we disappoint the Lord and embarrass his prophets, who are stating our case to world leaders (as to why we should be allowed to proselyte in their countries, for example), but also we leave the honorable people of the world without a model of how God would like his family to be organized on the earth in this final dispensation.

Sad to say, we live in a day when many live together unmarried, seeking sex and companionship without any commitment to marriage and parenthood. What an offense to our God! So many divorce and remarry, only to divorce again, destroying hopes, dreams, and the personal happiness of the innocent.

Same-gender "marriages" gain sympathetic support almost to legalization. Abortion is now a form of birth control for many. Permissiveness has reached hedonistic levels. We are reminded of the Savior's prophecy that our day would be like that of Noah's (see Matthew 24:37–39), when "every man" was "evil continually" (Moses 8:22).

Many years ago Elder John A. Widtsoe pinpointed our opportunities:

> Unless we give of ourselves we cannot build Zion, or anything else worthy of the great cause that the Lord has given us. . . . So we need, in this Church and Kingdom, for our own and the world's welfare, a group of men and women in their individual lives who shall be as a light to the nations, and rally standards for the world to follow. (D&C 45:9.) Such a people must be different from the world as it now is . . . unless the world has the same aim that we have. We are here to build Zion to almighty God, for the blessing of all the world. . . . We must respect that obligation, and not be afraid of it. We cannot walk as other men, or talk as other men, or do as other men, for we have a different destiny, obligation, and responsibility placed upon us, and we must fit ourselves for that great destiny and obligation. (*Conference Report,* April 1940:36.)

President Ezra Taft Benson gave us this perspective:

> For nearly six thousand years, God has held you in reserve to make your appearance in the final days before the second coming of the Lord. While our generation will be comparable in wickedness to the days of Noah, there is a major difference this time: God has saved for the final inning some of his strongest and most valiant children, who will help bear off the kingdom triumphantly. That is where you come in, for you are the generation that must be prepared to meet your God. . . . Make no mistake about it—you are a marked generation. There has never been more expected of the faithful in such a short period of time than there is of us. (Dedicatory Service, Boise LDS Institute of Religion, November 20, 1983.)

SUCCESSFUL MARRIAGES AND FAMILIES ARE CENTERED IN THE DOCTRINES OF THE GOSPEL

My purpose in this writing is to remind us of our divine mission in this final dispensation; to examine gospel perspectives that place marriage and family in their proper setting. This approach is based on the premise that understanding gospel doctrines and true principles are our best ally in strengthening our family life. Zion can only be established by "the principles of the law of the celestial kingdom" (D&C 105:5), by a people familiar with the eternal nature and importance of marriage and family in the plan of salvation. Therefore, I propose to discuss ten perspectives that I feel are essential if we are to establish more effective marriage and family practices among the Saints. I wholeheartedly adopt President Boyd K. Packer's premise "that the study of the doctrines of the gospel will improve behavior quicker than talking about behavior will improve behavior (*Ensign*, May 1997, p. 9).

If we build strong families God will honor us with peace and prosperity, and men and women of goodwill and decency will unite with us. The Lord promised that we would be impressive to those not of our faith: "Behold, if Zion [is faithful to her mission] she shall prosper, and spread herself and become very glorious, very great, and very terrible. And the nations of the earth shall honor her and shall say: Surely Zion is the city of our God, and surely Zion cannot fall, neither be moved out of her place, for God is there, and the hand of the Lord is there. . . . For this is Zion—THE PURE IN HEART." (D&C 97:18–19, 21.)

It has been almost two millennia since the Savior's ministry among the Nephites produced such a people, and even further back to the days of Enoch. But now, once again, we have in place the essential ingredients to replicate it: prophets, principles, priesthood keys and power, and a sufficient number of people committed to the task. We are on the right path. We can do it! We must do it, for we are under covenant so to do. Prophets of old eagerly looked to our day for us to accomplish that which they were unable to (see D&C 121:26–27).

1

The Most Important Work

Perspective One: We live in a period of time before the second coming of Jesus Christ, a time long-awaited by prophets from the days of Adam through John the Revelator. The Lord designated his Church at this time as "The Church of Jesus Christ of Latter-day Saints" (D&C 115:4). As we move toward the Millennium we must ask ourselves: "What is the most important work the Latter-day Saints could undertake at this time in this final dispensation?" The answer: Strong families!

THE RESTORATION

Consider the progress of the Church from its organization in 1830 to the present:

- We are no longer a small band of believers forced to move as outcasts because of friction with our neighbors.
- We are no longer being driven from county to county or having our homes burned to the ground by enemies.
- We are no longer draining mosquito-infested swampland to create new cities, or forced to cross deserts and plains in wagons or handcarts.
- We are not fleeing because of an extermination order.
- We are not giving birth to babies in the backs of wagons, burying family members in the frozen turf, dying of malaria, smallpox, or diphtheria, or freezing to death on

the plains, nor are we forced to eat sego lilies to survive in a mountain home.

- The legal system is no longer after us because of a supposed threat to constitutional law.
- Our missionaries, including mature couples, are allowed to go into most countries of the world to make friends and/or proselyte.
- Our fathers and sons are not leaving wives and families to join a Mormon Battalion.
- Our sons and fathers are not in the military in some faroff clime charging machine gun nests, storming beaches, attacking enemy positions, or dying of war-inflicted disease and injury.
- Husbands and fathers are no longer called to serve on missions while their wives and children remain at home.

The *Deseret News Church News* section reflects weekly the events of a worldwide church, a people who are gaining numerically and qualitatively throughout the world. In 1997 the Church reached the point at which there were more members living outside the United States than within. We are becoming a more established and respected people with each passing year. Prophets circle the globe meeting with the Saints and with governmental leaders in areas far from the Great Basin. Temples are beginning to dot the globe. Church leaders are interviewed on national television, and many people are coming to know something of the good works of the Church and its members; we have contributed much of our substance to the poor of the world. General conference addresses are beamed worldwide to Saints gathered in stake centers. All worthy men are eligible to hold and exercise the priesthood. Tens of thousands of missionaries teach the restored gospel throughout the earth.

With our rigorous pioneering in the United States behind us, a solid financial footing, and opportunities to reach parts of the world heretofore inaccessible, each of us must now ask the question I proposed earlier: What does the Lord expect of us now that our membership is growing so dramatically? What kind of pioneers are needed now to move the kingdom forward in the twenty-first century?

The answer to that query must come from the Lord's prophets, of course, and we need to consider their current counsel. They are telling us that God wants us to get on with the unfinished business of building Zion, of establishing a faithful people who will serve him, who will take the gospel to the world as well as to nearby friends and neighbors. We are to make gospel ordinances available to those on the other side of the veil. We are to be united as a people.

Our Father's desire, he confided to Enoch, is to have his children "love one another . . . [and] choose me, their Father" (Moses 7:33). The history of men and women from the days of Adam and Eve to the present gives evidence that most people have misunderstood the purpose of mortality. Former descendants of Jacob have not handled prosperity well, nor have they been the spiritual example that would draw others to the gospel. Israel was called to be the chosen people of the Lord, but their disobedience caused them to be cursed as outcasts, despised by others, and ultimately destroyed or scattered.

Unfortunately, Israel has imitated its captors and neighbors rather than be a people set apart as God's servants. Yet the Lord has not given them up; his promise is sure that if Zion gains sufficient spiritual strength she "shall prosper, and spread herself and become very glorious, very great. . . . And the nations of the earth shall honor her." (D&C 97:18–19.)

At this point in the dispensation, we are called by the title "Latter-day Saints." We must be capable of leading the world out of spiritual darkness in preparation for the return of the Messiah. We are to turn the Gentiles from the precipice of physical and spiritual destruction (see 1 Nephi 14:7), by providing them with an understanding of their potential as sons and daughters of a loving Heavenly Father committed "to bring to pass [their] immortality and eternal life" (Moses 1:39). But first, coming from a background of a false theology that does not view marriage and family as a long-term practice, they must see a model of marriage and family living as near perfect as possible if we are to get their attention. We must have our collective act together as a people.

President Brigham Young taught:

> The powers of earth and hell have striven to destroy this kingdom from the earth. The wicked have succeeded in doing so in former ages; but this kingdom they cannot destroy, because it is the last dispensation—because it is the fulness of times. It is the dispensation of all dispensations, and will excel in magnificence and glory every dispensation that has ever been committed to the children of men upon this earth. The Lord will bring again Zion, redeem his Israel, plant his standard upon the earth, and establish the laws of his kingdom, and those laws will prevail. (BY, *Journal of Discourses*, 8:36; hereafter cited as *JD*.)

From the watchtowers of Zion God's prophets have predicted the wonderful success and positive impact we can have on others if we will live the gospel. We have been promised that if we will live the gospel in our homes we can be a powerful influence to those who love their spouses and children and who want to be good companions and parents. Here is a favorite of mine: "I say to you Latter-day Saint mothers and fathers, if you will rise to the responsibility of teaching your children in the home—priesthood quorums preparing the fathers, the Relief Society the mothers—the day will soon be dawning when the whole world will come to our doors and will say, 'Show us your way that we may walk in your path'" (Micah 4:2). (Clyde Williams, ed., *The Teachings of Harold B. Lee* [Salt Lake City: Bookcraft, 1996], p. 277.)

President Spencer W. Kimball prophesied: "The time will come when only those who believe deeply and actively in the family will be able to preserve their families in the midst of the gathering evil around us" (*Ensign*, November 1980, p. 4). The value of his counsel is becoming more clear every day.

President Boyd K. Packer said that if we would live the gospel in our homes we would bring many into the kingdom: "Across the world, those who now [join the Church] by the tens of thousands will inevitably come as a flood to where the family is safe. Here they will worship the Father in the name of Christ, by the gift of the Holy Ghost, and know that the gospel is the great plan of happiness, of redemption, of which I bear witness." (*Ensign,* May 1994, p. 21.)

Such prophecies can only be fulfilled, of course, by a righteous people, a people who love the Lord, who love each other as husbands and wives, and where children grow up strong in the faith of their fathers, firm in a knowledge of the scriptures, and committed to their latter-day destiny. We must reach a state where divorce is practically unknown among us. Think of the impact we would have if our neighbors could observe: "I've never yet met a Mormon couple who divorced, and I live all around them. Surely they must break up their marriages, because it looks to me like everyone else does; but I have yet to see one." Or, if our neighbors could genuinely declare, "Those Mormons have big families, that's true. I don't know how they do it. But every one of their kids that I know is terrific. They are outgoing, social, friendly, they drop off hot bread regularly, stop in for a visit, shovel my walks in the winter, and if you hire one, they will give you your money's worth."

Our children, to make a difference in the days ahead, must be impressive by their competency and their example, for they must anchor a spiritual revival that will better the lives of all of God's family. Our homes must develop healthy and happy youngsters who can, in turn, attract worthy companions of their own, and then rear impressive children in the midst of unprecedented prosperity. When we are known more for the quality of our marriages and offspring than for the number of children, we will be making headway toward fulfilling these prophecies.

We have much to do. Our attention is needed in so many ways. Among Church members there has been a dramatic increase in the number of single parents in the last few decades. Far too many children are growing up without two parents to help them develop socially, mentally, and emotionally, who are capable of serving missions, succeeding at marriage, and establishing families of their own. Despite the heroic efforts of single moms and dads, children are best reared by two parents who are present and involved in their lives daily, two parents who love each other and set an example of affection and love in front of their children. Many years ago a prominent psychiatrist gave this perspective:

> The correct development of a child requires the commitment of mature parents who understand either consciously or intuitively that children do not grow up like Topsy. Good mothering from birth on provides the psychological core upon which all subsequent development takes place. Mothering is probably the most important function on earth. It is a full-time, demanding task. It requires a high order of gentleness, commitment, steadiness, capacity to give, and many other qualities, too. A woman needs a good man by her side so she will not be distracted and depleted, thus making it possible for her to provide rich humanness to her babies and children. Similarly, a good woman brings out the best in a man, who can then do his best for his wife and children. Children bring out the best in their parents. All together they make a family, a place where people of great strength are shaped, who in turn make strong societies. Our nation was built by such people.
>
> When the personalities of parents are crippled by psychological conflicts, in particular those which impair a clear sense of maleness or femaleness, or when children are deprived of the continuous commitment of mothers and fathers—especially mother—during the first few years of life, developmental disturbances occur in children of varying degrees of severity, depending on the time and duration of the parental absence or the degree of severity of the personality disturbances in the parents. The developmental disturbances in the children may show up in childhood, or they may go underground only to surface years later when life begins to make its demands on them—especially when they attempt to make families of their own. The most obvious consequence of disturbed childhood development is the inability to make lasting commitments. (Harold M. Voth, M.D. "The Family and the Future of America," in the *Alabama Journal of Medical Sciences,* vol. 15, no. 3 [July 1978], p. 310.)

That counsel still holds. Many today are afraid to make the commitment of marriage and would rather live together as couples without the responsibility of marriage.

Elder L. Tom Perry of the Quorum of the Twelve explained the challenge we face as more and more broken families find the gospel of Jesus Christ:

> Almost all of those who come for eternal marriages during the [coming decades] other than those few who will be coming from traditional homes, would not know the experience of growing up in a normal family. They will never have seen the proper relationship between a father and a mother, husband and wife, nor will they have had a proper home environment in which to live.
>
> [As Church members] we will have a great responsibility to help them understand correct principles, to direct them, and to teach them about traditional home values. People must be taught these essentials. Many children are now edging toward adulthood without seeing how the traditional home operates. Also, a large number of converts will be coming into the Church without traditional family backgrounds. . . . We will find ourselves standing pretty much alone [in the future] in the preservation of a family unit worthy to inherit the Celestial Kingdom . . . We must preserve the traditional family unit against all the destructive powers which are descending upon it. (LDS Social Services Conference, April, 1980, Church Office Building.)

All of us are living witnesses of teenage [Gadianton] gangs, drive-by shootings, increased drug use, bizarre dress and grooming, and vandalism coming from children and adolescents from broken homes. Too many youth are seeking greater thrills and performing more daring and repulsive acts of violence. Sexual impulses are being fanned by movies and television that portray ever more intimate behavior and revealing clothing, and children unacquainted with who they represent and their divine potential may be led astray by the popularity of movie stars, rock band leaders, and musical lyrics. In a day of ease and luxury it is easy, we learn from the Nephite example, to relax our vigil and for our children to grow up indifferent to spiritual matters (see Helaman 4:11–13, 22–25).

In our own day the Lord has chastised parents: "Now, I, the Lord, am not well pleased with the inhabitants of Zion, for there are idlers among them; and their children are also growing up in wickedness; they also seek not earnestly the riches of eternity, but their eyes are full of greediness. These things ought not to be and must be done away from among them." (D&C 68:31–32.)

President Gordon B. Hinckley told a member of the national press:

> The basic failure is in our homes. Parents haven't measured up to their responsibilities. It is evident. A nation will rise no higher than the strength of its homes. If you want to reform a nation, you begin with families, with parents who teach their children principles and values that are positive and affirmative and will lead them to worthwhile endeavors. That is the basic failure that has taken place in America. . . . Parents have no greater responsibility in this world than the bringing up of their children in the right way, and they will have no greater satisfaction as the years pass than to see those children grow in integrity and honesty and make something of their lives. (*Ensign*, November, 1996, pp. 48–49.)

WE ARE ACCOUNTABLE FOR OUR FAMILIES

God will hold us responsible for how well we carry out our marriage and family roles. President Spencer W. Kimball taught: "We shall all be judged and held accountable for how we carry out our various Church assignments, and our mortal stewardship will get no more searching scrutiny than with regard to the way we have served and loved our families and our sisters and brothers of the Church" (*Ensign*, November 1979, p. 49).

DIVORCE

To those who are struggling to stay in a marriage, the questions must be asked: "At what point is divorce justified?" "When would it be better to go on alone rather than to remain in a marriage that is obviously damaging personal dignity and spirituality?" Elder Boyd K. Packer answered that question in a general way:

> Even a rickety marriage will serve good purpose as long as two people struggle to keep it from falling down around them.
> . . . One who destroys a marriage takes upon himself a very great responsibility indeed. Marriage is sacred!
> To willfully destroy a marriage, either your own or that of another couple, is to offend our God. Such a thing will not be lightly considered in the judgments of the Almighty and in the eternal scheme of things will not easily be forgiven.
> Do not threaten nor break up a marriage. Do not translate some disenchantment with your own marriage partner or an attraction for someone else into justification for any conduct that would destroy a marriage. (*Ensign,* May 1981, p. 15.)

One of the questions that I have been asked many times, usually by a frustrated and discouraged wife, is "Would it not be better for me to divorce (or separate from) my husband so that my children will not have to grow up in an environment of fighting and contention?" I feel that if I concur, and say yes, I am encouraging divorce (or separation). If I reply no, I am saying that no harm will come to children exposed to family contention. The question is a difficult one when you see people suffer. The best answer I have found came from President Spencer W. Kimball: "Almost like a broken record come from divorcees that it is better to have [children] grow up in a single-parent home than a fighting home. The answer to that specious argument is: there need be no battling parents in fighting homes." (Edward L. Kimball, ed., *Teachings of Spencer W. Kimball* [Salt Lake City: Bookcraft, 1982], p. 314.)

Divorce or continued conflict are not the only options such married couples face. The best solution is to stop fighting; to behave as adults should, as they did when they thought marriage was the right answer. They need to rekindle the strengths they saw in each other years earlier; to realize that they are under covenant with God to support and sustain each other; and to realize how offensive contention, divorce, and destructive behavior is to God and the Spirit of the Lord. I believe that in nothing do we offend heaven more than when we belittle and abuse each other while we are under covenant to love and serve one another. No, couples and families who are fighting and quarrelling are not left with only the option to split up, to divide families. They have their agency to do so, of course, but they can do otherwise.[4] Conflict is not the Lord's way. The position on divorce was spelled out by Elder Joseph Fielding Smith:

> If all mankind would live in strict obedience to the gospel, and in that love which is begotten by the Spirit of the Lord, all marriages would be eternal, divorce would be unknown. Divorce is not part of the gospel plan and has been introduced because of the hardness of heart and unbelief of the people. . . .
>
> There never could be a divorce in this Church if the husband and wife were keeping the commandments of God. . . .
>
> A man would not get tired of his wife, if he had the love of God in his heart. A woman would not get tired of her husband if she had in her heart the love of God, that first of all commandments. They could not do it!
>
> . . . We have cases, perhaps, where a woman is justified in seeking relief, to be separated from a brutal husband who lives after the flesh, whose incontinency is such that he makes her life miserable; and they are not keeping the commandments that were given to them when they were married in the temple for time and all eternity, where he is supposed to love and respect and care for his wife with all the humility, in all the faith, and the understanding of the gospel of Jesus Christ. . . .
>
> Now I realize that there are some cases where a wife needs to have a separation, perhaps a husband should have a separa-

tion, but always because of a violation, a serious violation of the covenants that have been made.

If you want to know how serious it is to seek a divorce, . . . I want to tell you, people would be frightened rather than to seek a separation on some trivial matter. . . .

Marriage according to the law of the Church is the most holy and sacred ordinance. It will bring to the husband and the wife, if they abide in their covenants, the fullness of exaltation in the kingdom of God. When that covenant is broken, it will bring eternal misery to the guilty party, for we will all have to answer for our deeds done while in the flesh. It is an ordinance that cannot be trifled with, and the covenants made in the temple cannot be broken without dire punishment to the one who is guilty.

When a couple are married in the temple, they should try to live in peace and harmony, and if both are faithful members of the Church, this should not be impossible. Young people should try to tolerate each other's weaknesses and overcome them. If they live worthy of exaltation, they will enter the celestial kingdom without the frailties and weaknesses of mortality and will be perfect. (Bruce R. McConkie, ed., Joseph Fielding Smith, *Doctrines of Salvation,* [Bookcraft, 1955], vol. II, pp. 80–84.)

In a civilized society, of course, divorce performs an important outlet for the abused: separation from an adulterous spouse, physical and mental abuse, mean-spirited criticism and behavior, or the danger of becoming infected with a sexually transmitted disease brought home by a philandering spouse.

Though many divorces are justified, we must always be careful not to "release ourselves" from long-term marriage commitments without having made every effort to make changes in ourselves before we decide to end a marriage. President James E. Faust has given his opinion as to what constitutes a justifiable reason for divorce: "In my opinion," he said, "just cause should be nothing less serious than a prolonged and apparently irredeemable relationship which is destructive of a person's dignity as a human being." Then he explained that what most people consider adequate reasons for divorce are not justified in the eyes of God: "Surely it is not simply 'mental distress,' nor 'personality differences,' nor having 'grown apart,' nor having 'fallen out of love.' This is especially so where there are children." (*Ensign,* May 1993, pp. 36–37.)

BETTER PEOPLE, BETTER MARRIAGES

We can be no better spouses than we are as individuals. If changes are needed in our marriage, that change must first begin with us. We cannot make or force others to change; we can only work on our own behavior and attitude. Instead of blaming the culture as the primary culprit for broken families and unhappy marriage, we need to check our own hearts and behavior to ensure that we are not casting stones when it is our own skirts that are blood-stained. As Latter-day Saints we have a tendency sometimes to be so ethnocentric that we accuse those not of our faith of causing most of the social disruptions when we are capable of creating a great deal of mischief on our own. Hear a prophet of God, President Gordon B. Hinckley:

> We have wonderful people, but we have too many whose families are falling apart. It is a matter of serious concern, I think it is my most serious concern. I wish to see our people walk in the light of the Lord. That's where they will find their happiness, that's where they will find their progress, that's where they will find their prosperity, in walking the paths which the Lord has laid out for us. (*Church News,* June 7, 1995.)

If the biggest concern of a prophet is that of broken covenants and homes, then as Church members we need to seriously consider our marriage and parenting commitments, our family practices. We need to critically examine our relationship with our spouse and with each child. Those who are sarcastic, critical, overtly or subtly abusive are not only offending God but are jeopardizing their own salvation. Marriage is not two people perfect at living together, but rather two mortal, fallen, fallible, fumbling human beings proficient at repenting and at forgiving each other. The purpose of marriage is not to make two clones, but to respect the unique differences we possess as we travel the path to exaltation as a partnership.

2

Marriage and the Plan

Perspective Two: Marriage and family relations are strengthened most when we understand the place of marriage and family in the eternal plan of our Father.

Over the years I have observed that when marital or family problems arise, Church members will look everywhere but to the Lord, the prophets, or the application of gospel principles to resolve their difficulties. When it comes to the real life, too many of us think that we must look to the world's experts and scholars, its literature, its practitioners to find the most helpful answers to personal or family difficulties. Frequently the First Presidency feels compelled to warn the Saints to avoid workshops and seminars that promote the financial gain of the promoters but whose agenda does little to help improve marriages.

We need to understand this basic truth: Nothing is more helpful in strengthening marriage and family life than understanding the doctrine and living gospel principles. If that were not true, then some other approach would be the gospel of Jesus Christ.

The plan of salvation, together with the doctrines of the Restoration, covers every conceivable marital or family problem that could arise. That is not to suggest that we cannot benefit from the Lord's counsel, "seek ye out of the best books words of wisdom; seek learning, even by study and also by faith" (D&C 88:118), but the Church exists to help members gain exaltation, which is our ultimate goal. Therefore, does it not seem reasonable that the Lord would have the *best* answers by which to resolve our concerns in this most important area of our lives? In fact, scriptures and general conference talks are filled with help in shaping and changing our hearts and thus behavior to conform to eternal principles.

A colleague of mine, Brett Savage,[5] shared an experience with me concerning this very principle. Following his presentation at a marriage seminar, a woman came up to him and asked what he thought might be the best book to help her with a particular family difficulty. Brett picked up the Triple Combination (The Book of Mormon, the Doctrine and Covenants, and the Pearl of Great Price) and handed it to her. She replied: "Oh no, I don't mean that. I know about that. I mean something written recently that would really help in my situation." He again placed the scriptural volume in her hand. She repeated herself, saying she "wanted something more substantial"; that she "already knew about that book."

Contemporary Christians consider us non-Christians primarily because of our precepts on the Godhead, extra-biblical writings and revelation, grace and works—to us, fundamental gospel principles. We freely acknowledge that differences separate us from other denominations within the Christian tradition. The Lord's response to Joseph Smith in the First Vision to "join none of them" has set us on a different theological path. And nowhere is Latter-day Saint doctrine more unique than with regard to our position on marriage and family. Our teachings about men and women and eternal marriage constitute a completely different paradigm restored in our day because, the Lord said, "they have strayed from mine ordinances, and have broken mine everlasting covenant; they seek not the Lord to establish his righteousness, but every man walketh in his own way, and after the image of his own god" (D&C 1:15–16). In hopes of presenting the plan of salvation as an obvious problem-solver in our lives, let us review some important concepts of the family as they have been restored in our day.

1. *We lived as a family in the premortal life.* "All men and

women," the First Presidency declared, "are in the similitude of the universal Father and Mother, and are literally sons and daughters of Deity" (Heber J. Grant, Anthony W. Ivins, Charles W. Nibley, First Presidency, *Improvement Era,* vol. 13, pp. 75–81). Our Heavenly Father is our literal Father, a personal being in whose image men and women are created. He is the genetic parent of our spirit bodies. To be a husband and father, titles appropriate to him, requires a female counterpart. All men and women are the spirit offspring of heavenly parents, and we lived with them in a premortal first estate.[6] That makes us all brothers and sisters, a term we use frequently in Church settings.

Gender was part of our premortal heritage. "All human beings—male and female—are created in the image of God," said the First Presidency and Council of Twelve in the 1995 proclamation to the world. "Each is a beloved spirit son or daughter of heavenly parents, and, as such, each has a divine nature and destiny. Gender is an essential characteristic of individual premortal, mortal, and eternal identity and purpose." (President Gordon B. Hinckley, Proclamation on the Family, *Ensign,* November 1995, p. 101.)

As the literal spirit children of heavenly parents, we lived with them in a heavenly home before we came to this earth. Brigham Young explained:

> I want to tell you, each and every one of you, that you are well acquainted with God our heavenly Father, or the great Elohim. You are all well acquainted with Him, for there is not a soul of you but what has lived in His house and dwelt with Him year after year; and yet you are seeking to become acquainted with Him, when the fact is, you have merely forgotten what you did know. . . .
>
> There is not a person here today but what is a son or a daughter of that Being. In the spirit world their spirits were first begotten and brought forth, and they lived there with their parents for ages before they came here. This, perhaps, is hard for many to believe, but it is the greatest nonsense in the world not

to believe it. If you do not believe it, cease to call Him Father; and when you pray, pray to some other character. (*JD* 4:216.)

In that premortal sphere we were born and grew to be adult spirits. However, we did not marry or possess the power of procreation at that point in our existence. Our heavenly parents, not unlike mortal parents, wanted their mature children to progress to the same state that they had reached. The plan of salvation calls for children to move "out of the house" to learn for themselves principles that can only be mastered independent of parental supervision. This earth was therefore created as a place where the family of God could come to the "school of mortality," a school whose curricula leads to exaltation. It has to be a place where good and evil can exist side by side. That was not possible in heaven (D&C 1:31), for rebellion would result in being cast out of God's presence. There have been many who have passed through this schooling before us and many more will come after us. It has been the eternal plan. The prophet Joseph Smith taught:

God himself was once as we are now, and is an exalted man, and sits enthroned in yonder heavens! That is the great secret. If the veil were rent today, and the great God who holds this world in its orbit, and who upholds all worlds and all things by his power, was to make himself visible—I say, if you were to see him today, you would see him like a man in form—like yourselves in all the person, image, and very form as a man; for Adam was created in the very fashion, image and likeness of God, and received instruction from, and walked, talked and conversed with him, as one man talks and communes with another. (Joseph Fielding Smith, comp., *Teachings of the Prophet Joseph Smith*, Salt Lake City: Deseret Book, p. 345. Hereafter cited as TPJS.)

We assume that our heavenly parents passed through experiences similar to our own, possessing mortal bodies, experiencing death and resurrection, a state of being forever immortal. They live in a glorified and exalted state of marriage and family relationships. That, of course, is how we came to be their spirit children, offspring of wonderful parents who gained their exaltation long ago and became the creators of our spirit bodies. Our ultimate goal therefore as their children is to attain to that same level of perfection in the eternities that they have achieved. The mission of Jesus Christ enables us to progress to that same stature. That becomes possible when we are resurrected with a male or a female body and where death is no longer possible. (See Alma 11:45; D&C 138:17.)

Because our Heavenly Father and his Son (and to a great extent our own mortal parents) know from firsthand experience what we feel and think, they love us dearly and know how to succor and nurture us in our mortal setting. Our Eternal Father has given us commandments so we will not "play hooky" or procrastinate in passing the curriculum. He knows the desires of our hearts (see D&C 137:9), and understands the feelings and challenges we face here. Elder Neal A. Maxwell reminded us of the Savior's love and his knowledge of what we are passing through:

> Can we, even in the depths of disease, tell Him anything at all about suffering? . . . Can those who yearn for hearth or home instruct Him as to what it is like to be homeless or on the move? . . . Can we really counsel Him about being misrepresented, misunderstood, or betrayed? . . . Can we educate Him regarding injustice or compare failures of judicial systems with the Giver of the Law, who, in divine dignity, endured its substantive and procedural perversion? And when we feel so alone, can we presume to teach Him who trod "the wine-press alone" anything at all about feeling forsaken? . . . Do we presume to instruct Him in either compassion or mercy? . . . Can we excuse our compromises because of the powerful temptations of status seeking? . . . Can we lecture Him on liberty. . . . Can those concerned with nourishing the poor advise Him concerning feeding the multitudes? . . . Can those who are concerned with medicine instruct Him about healing the sick? . . . Or can we inform the Atoner about feeling the sting of ingratitude when

one's service goes unappreciated or unnoticed? . . . Should we seek to counsel Him in courage? Should we rush forth eagerly to show Him our mortal medals—our scratches and bruises— He who bears His five special wounds? . . . Indeed, we cannot teach Him anything! But we can listen to Him. We can love Him, we can honor Him, we can worship Him! We can keep His commandments, and we can feast upon His scriptures! (*Ensign*, November 1981, pp. 8–9.)

2. *Marriage and family is the central focus of the Atonement and the plan of salvation.* Latter-day Saints see the Atonement as the key to eternal marriage. The gift of the atonement of Jesus Christ restores men and women to a male or female body incapable of death again. Exaltation consists in becoming like our heavenly parents—resurrected, immortal, and possessing the ability to use procreative powers even in that glorified state. All others live in a lesser degree of glory.

3. *A celestial or temple marriage is the gate leading to exaltation.* To obtain eternal life a man and woman must enter into an order of priesthood, the new and everlasting covenant of marriage (see D&C 131:1–4). Then they must keep the covenants and obligations associated with their marriage. These ordinances allow a couple sealed in the temple to be husband and wife not only in this life but in the spirit world and in the highest degree of resurrected glory, which will be here upon this earth in its celestial state (see D&C 88:20).

4. *There are lower orders of marriage.* In mortality men and women may be honorably married by civil authority/statute. Such marriages are temporary in nature, "until death do you part," but essential because not all individuals are members of the Church nor are all members worthy of the highest marriage available in the temple. Such individuals marry until death overtakes them (or we activate or convert them to obtain a temple sealing).

5. *Divorce is not part of the gospel plan.* Divorce was never intended to end a marriage, whether it was a temple marriage or that of a secular authority. Because of wickedness and hard-heartedness, however, men and women do not always live gospel

standards and therefore divorce is permitted where either abuse or sin destroys the affection of one or both spouses. To obtain a divorce, a couple applies through legal channels in the secular courts. The Lord's system allows for a "cancellation of sealing" through the living prophet; innocent parties are then free to marry again in the temple. Under ideal conditions, divorce is only permitted where sexual sins are involved (see Matthew 19:7–9).[7]

Our understanding of the eternal nature of marriage and family provides the incentive and motivation to become like our heavenly parents and establish good marriage and family practices.[8] Elder Boyd K. Packer made this point explicit in saying that "the study of the doctrines of the gospel will improve behavior quicker than a study of behavior will improve behavior. . . . That is why we stress so forcefully the study of the doctrines of the gospel." (*Ensign*, November 1986, p. 17.)

3

Doctrines Can Change Behavior

Perspective Three: Doctrine can change our behavior in ways more powerful and long-lasting than secular principles can.

The Power of Doctrine

If understanding true doctrine is the key to marital happiness, as the prophets have taught us, then we need to look more specifically to how and what doctrines can improve marital stability and marital satisfaction. Consider how the following doctrines provide marriage and family perspectives with power to change our behavior to conform to heavenly principles:

1. *We came to the earth to obtain a body of flesh and bones, to be tested and tried in the endowment of flesh, in an arena of choice between good and evil.* We were removed from the presence of God to experience two opposites, good and evil, for we cannot be exalted without understanding both concepts. The Lord declared: "I the Lord cannot look upon sin with the least degree of allowance" (D&C 1:31). Yet when Adam and Eve fell, the Lord declared, "Behold, the man is become as one of us, to know good and evil" (Genesis 3:22). God is God not because he does not know what evil is. He understands it better than anyone. But as Lehi explained, "it must needs be that there was an opposition," for "man could not act for himself save it should be that

he was enticed by the one or the other" (2 Nephi 2:15–16). Hence this life was established as one whereby we could gain experience in matters of law, agency, and consequences.

2. *Marriage and parenthood.* In mortal life we marry and become parents. We seek a companion to be an eternal spouse.[9] Temples allow us to participate in sealing ordinances that enable us to organize a family. Our task as a married couple then becomes one of helping each other attain exaltation by learning, teaching, and providing a home together where we may practice and develop Christlike traits. Marriage is the most intimate relationship we experience in mortality and it is there that we teach and learn from each other how to live gospel principles in order to inherit eternal glory. In effect, we agree to take each other on as a "project" to gain exaltation!

President Spencer W. Kimball counseled: "In selecting a companion for life and for eternity, certainly the most careful planning and thinking and praying and fasting should be done to be sure that of all the decisions, this one must not be wrong. In true marriage there must be a union of minds as well as of hearts. Emotions must not wholly determine decisions, but the mind and the heart, strengthened by fasting and prayer and serious consideration, will give one a maximum chance of marital happiness." ("Marriage and Divorce," BYU Devotional, September 7, 1976, pp. 2–3.)

This life was set up for us to accomplish a number of things for the Father's family:

3. *The Atonement can exalt married couples.* Our Father, knowing that we would err, foreordained a Savior as part of the plan, one that could redeem his children from sin that carries an eternal penalty—being cast out of the Father's presence forever. The central and most important event in all eternity is the offering that Jesus Christ gave to each of us upon conditions of repentance and acceptance of the Father's gospel. Without his blood being shed in our behalf and his coming forth from the grave, not only would our sins damn us but we would remain spirits forever, negating marriage and family. We would return to living as spirits like we were in the premortal life, as Satan must

be forever; without a body that combines spirit and element that enable us to experience a fulness of joy (see D&C 93:33–34). Thus we would be ineligible for eternal life and exaltation. The Savior's life and death provided the way for us to receive the following blessings:

- Forgiveness of sins
- Resurrection of the physical body and its joining forever with the spirit body as an immortal soul (D&C 88:14–15)
- Retention of male and female attributes and traits in our resurrected bodies
- Continuation of relationships formed by priesthood authority—God's authority—after death and into the post-resurrection eternity
- Marriage covenants between faithful partners remaining valid beyond death
- Temple and priesthood ordinances uniting us together forever as families
- An assurance of exaltation while we are yet mortal
- Joint-heirship with Christ and inheritance of all that the Father possesses (D&C 84:38)
- Living on this earth, which will be a future celestial kingdom (D&C 88:20)
- Eternal lives as exalted, glorified, resurrected, and noble couples (D&C 131:1–4)

4. *Satan's curse and damnation is that he will never marry or become the head of a posterity.* Satan's most serious curse other than being cast out of the presence of the Father is his inability to marry or become a father. Orson Pratt explained:

Could wicked and malicious beings, who have eradicated every feeling of love from their bosoms, be permitted to propagate their species, the offspring would partake of all the evil, wicked, and malicious nature of their parents. . . . It is for this reason that God will not permit the fallen angels to multiply; it is for this reason that God has ordained marriages for the righteous only [in eternity]; it is for this reason that God will put a final

stop to the multiplication of the wicked after this life: it is for
this reason that none but those who have kept the celestial law
will be permitted to multiply after the resurrection. ("Celestial
Marriage," *The Seer*, October 1853, p. 157.)

The notion that marriage and parenthood ceases at death, an
idea prominent in our day, originated with Satan, the father of
lies. Because he must remain celibate and impotent forever, he is
determined that "all men might be miserable like unto himself"
(2 Nephi 2:27). For one who loves spouse and children, to be
limited in their association for the brief period of mortality
would represent the worst possible aspect akin to hell and
damnation (D&C 131:1–4).

Because Satan is denied these powers and privileges, he is determined to undermine and destroy those who do marry, especially those who are under covenant through a temple sealing.
His greatest efforts are designed to prevent us from having an
eternal marriage.

5. *As God's children we are preparing now for the kind of life
that God lives.* As God's offspring we have the potential to reach
an exalted state if we adhere to the plan laid out for us. The First
Presidency explained our potential:

> So far as the stages of eternal progression and attainment have
> been made known through divine revelation, we are to under-
> stand that only resurrected and glorified beings can become
> parents of spirit offspring. Only such exalted souls have reached
> maturity in the appointed course of eternal life; and the spirits
> born to them in the eternal worlds will pass in due sequence
> through the several stages or estates by which the glorified par-
> ents have attained exaltation. (First Presidency, 30 June 1916,
> in James R. Clark, ed., *Messages of the First Presidency*,
> Bookcraft, 1971, 5:34.)

Because resurrected beings cannot die (see Alma 11:45;
D&C 138:17), eternal marriage is possible for those who qualify
for the highest degree of glory in the celestial kingdom (D&C
131:1–4).

DIVORCE-PROOFING OUR MARRIAGES

When we view marriage from these eternal doctrinal concepts we see marriage and family as the most profound experiences of our eternal existence. The date we marry becomes a date on the celestial calendar, like birth, baptism, and death. It has a profound influence on what we are and what we may become. Divorce is not pleasing to God. It is a major plague of our day. When we divorce we are proving to our Heavenly Father that we cannot live the higher principles of the gospel of Jesus Christ—at least at the time we divorce.[10] Recall that the Savior admonished the Pharisees that divorce comes because of the "hardness of your hearts." In the days of Moses and Christ, men could divorce their wives for minor reasons (see Deuteronomy 24:1–4). In the Church today one who honorably obtains a divorce is free to marry again without the stain of adultery spoken of in Matthew 19:9 and Matthew 5:32.

Elder Bruce R. McConkie wrote:

> Divorce is not a part of the gospel plan no matter what kind of marriage is involved. But because men in practice do not always live in harmony with gospel standards, the Lord permits divorce for one reason or another, depending upon the spiritual stability of the people involved. In ancient Israel men had power to divorce their wives for relatively insignificant reasons. (Deuteronomy 24:1–4.) Under the most perfect conditions there would be no divorce permitted except where sex sin was involved. In this day divorces are permitted in accordance with civil statutes, and the divorced persons are permitted by the Church to marry again without the stain of immorality which under a higher system would attend such a course. (*Doctrinal New Testament Commentary*, vol. 1, Bookcraft, 1965, p. 547.)

Divorce destroys family life and comes about among Church members because of the carelessness and indifference of men and women to each other when one or both stop living gospel principles. The breakup of marriage indicates a lack of spiritual maturity by one or both partners.

I recall a General Authority who toured my mission telling me that he had to release a man from an important ecclesiastical position because "he wants to divorce his wife." "I told him," this authority confided to me, "that you don't do that after you have served in the Church positions you have—elder's quorum president, bishop, stake president." I took his point to be that when an individual has been in positions of ecclesiastical trust, has himself counseled others with marital difficulties, has taught to others the basic doctrines of the gospel (including the importance of marriage and family), has listened, examined, and judged the behavior of those who broke marriage covenants, has sermonized to those who proposed the same thing he was now choosing—that he, above all others, should understand that divorce has no place in the lives of spiritually mature people.

Individuals seeking a divorce (not justified by the Lord) have somehow missed the significance of marriage and family in the eternal plan. "I told him," the authority explained, "that not only would I have to release him from his Church position if he pursued that course, but more importantly, he was placing his own salvation in jeopardy. He would have some difficult questions to answer at the Judgment. How would he explain his decision to break his marriage vows to the Final Judge?" Covenant-breaking is a serious spiritual offence.

APPLICATION OF GOSPEL PRINCIPLES

If a husband truly understood these basic doctrines, how could he not desire to become the best husband and father possible? What wife who understood her divine role as wife and mother would not want to be her best self in order to reach her divine potential? What couple would not eagerly anticipate parenthood when given the privilege?

Elder Packer was right. Doctrine is a powerful incentive to keep us on track and to keep our marriages and parenting practices in harmony with eternal principles. It is doctrine that reveals to men and women their divine possibilities as husbands and wives, as fathers and mothers in the plan of salvation. It is doctrine that brings about a desire to bring our behavior into compliance with these eternal principles. Here in mortality we apprentice on a small scale what God is able to do on one much grander in scope. When we view our spouse as our eternal companion, confidante, lover, the mother or father of our children, and our personal therapist, we gain an appreciation for him or her that builds feelings of love and emotions capable of transcending death. All our dying does is move us to a different venue to continue the great love affair we began here in mortality. These feelings do not change because our spirit body steps out of its mortal counterpart.

Would any happily married person worship a God who designed some other plan? Consider a plan that has us come to earth, gain a mortal body, where we are commanded to marry and bear children—and then, after years in these profound family relationships, could we be expected to lose these feelings and ties because of death? Of course not! Cherishing our emotional affiliations and experiences with each other, I think we would be angry with God if marriage and family associations ended at death. What an irrational plan that would be to inflict on men and women when it has already been proven that death could be overcome. Jesus Christ was resurrected and we are all the beneficiaries. One person came back to life, proving to us that we live forever. The grave is only a temporary victory over death, a short separation for a couple.

The Savior was resurrected with the same gender attributes he possessed before death, and so will we be. He expressed tender feelings for Mary at the tomb, indicating that we retain our sensitivity. He remained a man. How un-Godlike it would be to lose our identity simply because we die. People who believe such an idea are unaware of the meaning and implications of the atonement of Jesus Christ.

Yes, there are requirements of personal worthiness if we are to retain these relationships—that is understood; but if the atonement of Jesus Christ has not the power to restore resurrected male and female bodies *and* family associations after death, then what is the purpose of mortality? Who would worship the God of that plan? People under that plan would live in constant fear of mortality cutting family associations short. The death of loved ones would be tragic under such a program. Every honest soul would question God if they did not rebel against him as did Satan.

Surely we would ask: "Why would a being who knows all things and who has all power set up such a useless and wasteful plan?" "Why did I marry, only to lose my family in death?" "I had a number of children and loved them dearly," we would argue. "Why can I not now know them and be with them as I was before? What was the purpose of Jesus' ministry anyway?" Our questioning of God's purposes would be endless.

RESURRECTION AND RESTORATION

I am convinced that the specific doctrine that has the most power to influence our behavior as companions and parents is that of the resurrection or, as I see it, the restoration of the soul. The resurrection welds bodies of flesh and bone to a spirit body so that the combination can no longer die or be separated. And that body retains its gender. These two concepts—immortality and gender—open the door to understanding how marriage and family can be eternal. Then when you add righteousness as a condition for exaltation, you have the complete formula of doctrine and attitude coming together.

When a couple is sealed by priesthood authority (the authority of an eternal being), then death does not negate marriage, gender, our bodies, or sealings. If we are faithful to our covenants we not only remain husband and wife in the spirit world following mortality but also we continue as married couples in the resurrection. That is the gift of the Atonement to those who treat each other as they should. The priesthood key to perform sealings was restored by Elijah on April 3, 1836, to the Prophet Joseph Smith in the Kirtland Temple (see D&C 110:13).

If marriage and family life were only short-term, for-this-life-only, till-death-do-us-part experiences (the prevailing theological notion), then it would be easy to understand why so many marriage and family tragedies abound. Were marriage and family life limited to this short mortal blip on the eternal screen, individuals could justify perhaps, to some extent, the behavior that is so evident in our society: serial marriage and divorce and marriage again as Hollywood characters are wont to do; one spouse deserting the other for one more attractive or compatible at the moment; aberrant lifestyles; treating physical bodies as poster boards (body rings and piercing come to mind). Brutality, abuse, celibacy, domestic partnerships, living together without marriage, abortion on demand, limiting family size, postponing children or avoiding parenthood altogether—these are easily justified and all too common phenomena in our present culture.

The only way such behavior could be entertained and accepted by rational beings, it seems to me, is to believe that life is a cosmic accident, a product of some evolutionary luck. Either God does not exist, or he doesn't really care what we do or how we treat each other or our bodies, or life is so uncertain that there are no standards to live by. In such a belief system, behavioral imperatives would be practically non-existent; individual wants and needs would drive behavior; situational ethics would prevail over doctrinal standards. If God were simply a spirit, a being without body, parts, or passions, what difference would marriage and family make anyway? When you think about it, does anyone worry about doctrine anymore?

To Latter-day Saints, if God were some spirit essence that fills space or a being who has not spoken for almost two millennia, it would be easy for people to "do their own thing" without worrying about eternal consequences. God would be only an imaginary character, like Santa Claus, who gets everyone's wish list but which must be carried out by our own ingenuity and effort. That kind of thinking would lead to individuals who were self-sufficient, smug; who admired their own conceit. Each individual would be on his own to decide what was best for himself or herself.

The Lord told Joseph Smith, "They seek not the Lord to establish his righteousness, but every man walketh in his own way,

and after the image of his own god, whose image is in the likeness of the world" (D&C 1:16). Of course, all agree that legal
boundaries are needed to preserve private property and freedoms. It is agreed that there must be limits if a civilized society
is to survive. Social and legal sanctions must be in place, for
wealth and prosperity are of no value if robbers and thieves can
take them at will. Police, lawyers, and the courts are necessary.
But other than for legal infractions, tolerance has become the
governing rule for adult behavior. "That's just the way it is."
"Whatever consenting adults decide to do in private is their own
business," come the refrains. "If people choose different living
arrangements than you do, what is that to you?" "Whose business *could* it be but theirs?"

Anyone daring to criticize adults in their personal and private
life is considered un-educated, arrogant, a right-wing religious
fanatic, irrationally opinionated, and/or out of touch with reality. We have come to the point where everyone wants to "do
their own thing" with no guilt or standards of decency except
their own personal views (shades of Korihor—see Alma 30). No
questioning of immorality.

Satan is very clever. In this last dispensation, he has inspired
theologians to make God an impersonal spirit essence that fills
the universe. Such "doctrine" allows people to satisfy their own
wills. If God is not a personal God, there is nothing to fear. Did
not Nephi see that attitude in vision of "eat, drink, and be
merry" for our day; "nevertheless, fear God—he will justify in
committing a little sin; yea, lie a little, take the advantage of one
because of his words . . . there is no harm in this; and do all
these things, for tomorrow we die; and if it so be that we are
guilty, God will beat us with a few stripes, and at last we shall be
saved in the kingdom of God." Then he says, "Yea, and there
shall be many which shall teach after this manner" (2 Nephi
28:8–9).

Without a belief in a personal God who will someday pass
judgment on our choices, or one who has clearly defined marriage, or one who is offended by immoral behavior, or one who
has given specific laws—without such a belief people feel free to

do as they please and ignore divine injunctions.[11] This perspective reached a crescendo in an earlier day when God declared to Enoch that the people had gone "astray, and have denied me, and have sought their own counsels in the dark; and in their own abominations have they devised murder, and have not kept the commandments, which I gave unto [them]" (Moses 6:28).

President Boyd K. Packer explained:

> The word *tolerance* is also invoked as though it overrules everything else. Tolerance may be a virtue, but it is not *the* commanding one. There is a difference between what one *is* and what one *does*. What one is may deserve unlimited tolerance; what one does, only a measured amount. A virtue when pressed to the extreme may turn into a vice. Unreasonable devotion to an ideal, without considering the practical application of it, ruins the ideal itself. (*Ensign,* November 1990, p. 85.)

Few, it seems, agree on what is right or wrong behavior. Variant forms of marriage and family life have thus come into being, labeled by adherents as "growth-promoting," or "realistic," or "social experiments," or "a cultural phenomenon" or "that's just the way people do it these days." "Hey—this is a free country," and freedom rules. Without an eternal perspective, even family scientists are limited to observing, interviewing, measuring, describing, surveying, and drawing correlations and conclusions; no "thou shalts" or "shalt-nots."

Here is an example of what happens when tolerance becomes the ruling standard:

> Administrators at the University of California at Berkeley were paralyzed for months over what to do about the behavior of "the Naked Guy." In the fall of 1992, a student . . . made a practice of walking around the campus in the nude. He jogged, ate in the dining halls, and attended classes while totally naked. When asked why he wore no clothes, he said he was protesting sexually repressive traditions in Western society. Female students were uncomfortable in his presence, and both males and

females were nervous about the "seat issue"—not wanting to sit where he had recently sat.

It is unbelievable that it took the Cal administrators all fall and winter to deal with this outrage. They couldn't come up with a legal excuse or a school regulation that would require "the Naked Guy" to either suit up or ship out. Instead, every precaution was taken not to violate his rights. . . . Finally in late January [1993], [he] was sent packing. How did they finally get him out? Some female students charged that his behavior constituted "sexual harassment"! That says it all, doesn't it? The man was not expelled for violating established standards of decency. He had to trip over a tenet of political correctness before he could be thrown out on his naked rear end.

[Apparently the student] is now preparing a lawsuit against the university. That figures. Hard-pressed Californians paid taxes to give this ungrateful dude an education, and he threw it in their faces." (Bob Greene, "What Does the Naked Guy Tell Us About Our Society?" *Dallas Morning News,* February 14, 1993, p. 7J.)

Prophets work differently. They speak out in direct opposition to the philosophies of men, who live by a mortality-limited creed. Prophets, on the other hand, are accountable to God to declare the truth fearlessly and boldly (see D&C 112:30–33). God's wisdom and that of his prophets come from an eternal perspective rather than from short-term expediency.

SATAN'S PLAN DID NOT INCLUDE FAMILY

If in the premortal council Satan had argued in behalf of a continuation of marriage and parenthood after mortal life and *then* his plan had been rejected, we might understand why so many joined him in his revolt against the Father. But such was not the case. Not only was he more interested in power and glory than in service and love, but also he will remain an impotent bachelor forever. What a terrible price to pay for arrogance and pride! Thus bereft, he "seeketh that all men might be miserable like unto himself" (2 Nephi 2:27).

The plan of salvation is much more farsighted. One of the important parts of the mission of Jesus Christ was to see that marriage and family life continues forever.

Sometimes it is easier to appreciate a concept when it is contrasted with its opposite. Consider these two perspectives: (1) marriage and family life are temporary, mortal phenomena, (2) marriage and family life are eternal.

If marriage is for this life only, may we not logically comment:
- Why marry at all?
- What's wrong with abortion?
- Are children really necessary in order for us to be fulfilled? Of course, sexual drives need to be satisfied. Okay, but why children? With birth control, there is no need to have children. Okay, if a "maternal instinct" exists in my partner, we may want to see if we can have children; but not until after we settle down and get our careers well on their way. We don't want to hurt our marriage by having children before we are ready.
- Priorities center around careers, money, possessions, home, cars, computers, the Internet—material things.
- Divorce is unfortunate, but if things don't work out or if either one or both partners are not happy, life is too short to remain in an unhappy marital situation.
- Purpose of life? Not clear.
- Affection: "Whatever feels good—do it!"
- Live together before marriage? Of course. A trial marriage is necessary to check out compatibility—especially the sexual role.
- Life gravitates toward *self*. It is "my" happiness that counts.
- Decisions are ultimately made by the wage earner, by the oldest, or by the one with the most education.

- Sexual standard: anything goes, whether before or after marriage.
- Religion? Let the children make their own decisions as they mature. They should decide their own beliefs and destiny.
- Solutions to marital problems come through trained professionals—not through priesthood leaders or God's inspiration.

On the other hand, consider marriage and family life through the lenses of an eternal perspective.

MARRIAGE CAN LAST FOREVER

- The atonement of Jesus Christ provides a resurrection for us as male and female and thus opens the way for husband and wife to be eternal companions. This is the most glorious news in all eternity for married lovers. Death is not the end of marriage and family life.
- We want to be our very best selves so that we can attract an eternal companion, consummate marriage, and bear and rear healthy children who are the spirit children of God; or be our very best selves so that our spouse is grateful that we are married and we are under covenant together.
- Family backgrounds prepare us for marriage, and we seek a companion with values similar to our own. We want to establish the best environment for our children to grow up in so as to prepare them to succeed in their own marriages.
- Careful and wise dating, only at an appropriate age, is important so as to prevent immaturity and inexperience from spoiling our potential.
- LDS missions are critical for young men, who will need to provide materially and spiritually for their future families.

- Temple marriage provides the only way for an eternal relationship to continue beyond mortality.
- Each has a personal desire and commitment to be the best person one can be as a son or daughter of God, to please him and to be worthy of being in his presence again.
- We have a desire to repent or apologize when we offend spouse or child.
- We readily forgive spouse/children when they err.
- Spiritual solutions resolve problems best: Prayer is essential, scriptures keep hearts softened; prophets and Apostles teach us how to avoid modern pitfalls.
- We become Christlike in heart and motives as we "come unto Christ"; we exercise charity with love and compassion and respect for those we love.
- Equal partnership—we are in this adventure together as a couple. Neither one can make it alone, so how we treat each other is important to our happiness here and preparation for eternity.
- Charity/compassion/respect/love—Christlike traits are essential to resolve differences as we come to appreciate our unique personalities and find we don't agree on everything.
- Sex is sacred, eternal in nature—so we will learn from and teach each other.
- We seek feedback on how to please one another, how we can improve in our marriage roles, and we will give gentle, kind instruction when adjustments/changes are needed and be humble in receiving correction.
- We return to the temple often to renew our covenants and foster eternal perspectives.
- We use fast Sundays to seek personal revelation on how to be a better spouse and companion.
- We date as often as possible; enrich our marriage and family life; have frequent talks about our marriage and family progress.
- Family home evenings become opportunities to build relationships.

This may be the most obvious demonstration of how doctrine affects behavior directly. Understanding our potential as "forever families," we will ensure that our behavior conforms to the doctrinal framework. We can judge our own behavior and that of others by how we measure up to the plan. Without doctrines and principles to orient our thinking, behavior degenerates.

RATIONALIZING BEHAVIOR

In the context of the gospel perspective, we are better prepared to evaluate the events in our society. How often do we shake our heads in disbelief at what we read and see in the daily news. I have listened to people explain their unusual behavior in their relationships by what to them is logical and reasonable; a "trial marriage," for example. Without a gospel perspective, such a relationship seems plausible to many. A high divorce rate scares people away from marriage, and they think that imitating marriage has merit. Many selfishly try to answer nature's mating call while avoiding the responsibility. I listened to a homosexual person argue that God will allow him in the celestial kingdom with a same-gender spouse because "He understands our feelings." Indeed, doctrine gives us a different set of lenses to use in analyzing behavior in our contemporary society.

LATTER-DAY SAINT RESPONSE

Without being condescending, condemning, or uncharitable, we can be capable Latter-day Saints living gospel principles. We can light the path and show others the way to better family living through example and confirming research. There are many good and decent people in the world who possess light and truth and common sense (see D&C 123:12–13). Latter-day Saints are not the sole proprietors of decency and right thinking, and many of our neighbors will respond to our leadership in the family arena. In this way, every member is truly a missionary for the Lord's plan.

We don't stick our heads in the sand and ignore current trends in the secularization of the family because of our charity. We can be more questioning of research that comes to conclusions contrary to the Lord's counsel. For example, research may report that the children of working mothers are, if not superior, at least equal in social, moral, and intellectual development to those children with stay-at-home-mothers. And of course individual children and families will experience a variety of outcomes. Yet the Lord through his prophets has been clear that mothers can best serve their children by spending time with them.

Studies of children growing up with a homosexual father and his domestic partner, or a lesbian mother and her female companion, report that the children of these couples were just as well adjusted as children who come from traditional homes! The gospel perspective makes one suspicious of such findings. In time, of course, good research will sort out what is and what isn't accurate. Hopefully, Church members trained in the social sciences will spot weak research and point out the fallacies of poorly designed studies to a world too gullible if it hears the words "research shows," or "studies prove."

Dr. Randal Wright's research, on the other hand, confirmed what President Ezra Taft Benson called for several years back concerning mothers being "at the crossroads" when children come home from school and dates.[12] His research suggested that the most typical time of day for sexual activity to occur between teens who engage in immoral behavior is between three and five o'clock in the afternoon. The most typical place for such acts to take place is at the home of one teen or the other. When truth is revealed by the Lord through living prophets, such wisdom can guide research; in fact, our social science departments at Brigham Young University and other Church schools frequently confirm what the Lord has already revealed to be accurate (see Brent Top and Bruce Chadwick, *Rearing Righteous Youth of Zion,* Bookcraft, 1998). Where the Lord has been silent, we search out of the best books and do our best thinking, always guided by the basic tenets of the plan of salvation.

The doctrines of the plan of salvation cause us to monitor our behavior more than just talking, researching, observing, and thinking about it. The motivation to do better, to be better, to behave better, comes from understanding our eternal potential as sons and daughters of God.

SUMMARY

Gospel doctrine inspires us to be more effective companions and parents. President Gordon B. Hinckley summarized the components that comprise healthy family patterns:

> Strong family life comes of strong and clear religious under-standing of who we are, and why we are here, and of what we may eternally become. Strong family life comes of the percep-tion that each of us is a child of God, born with a divine birthright, and with a great and significant potential. Strong family life comes of parents who love and respect one another, and who love and respect and nurture their children in the ways of the Lord. These are undergirding principles of our teachings as a church. To the degree that we observe these teachings we build strong families whose generations will strengthen the na-tion. (*Ensign,* November 1990, p. 54.)

4

Our Father Cares

Perspective Four: We are in Heavenly Father's family; he cares about each one of us and is anxious to assist us in gaining exaltation.[13]

"The doctrine of the family begins with heavenly parents. Our highest aspiration is to be like them." (Elder Robert D. Hales, *Ensign*, November 1996:94.)[14]

Heavenly Father wants us to succeed.[15] However, once children have agency and move away from home, they often make choices inconsistent with what the parents would want them to choose. We all make mistakes. We all misjudge. And Satan makes it doubly difficult for us to make correct decisions all the time because of his insistent temptations. This plan of the Father would be very dangerous if it were not for the atonement of Jesus Christ, which covers the mistakes and sins of which we repent. It is an ingenious plan, the curriculum of godhood.[16]

We left our premortal home to come to this earth to be tested in agency, laws, and decency. It is important to our Father that we return home honorably, prepared to assume the obligations of spiritual adulthood we call exaltation. President Harold B. Lee explained what should be our greatest fear as mortals:

> Now, the only fear we ought to have in this world is the fear of losing our place in the eternal family circle. That's all we ought to be afraid about. And the greatest deterrent to evil, if you understand rightly, is the fear that you might make some

mistake in an unguarded moment that might forbid you, except
through repentance—or perhaps if you can't repent, then forbid you forever—from attaining to the fullness of that family
blessing which otherwise could be yours. That's all you have to
be concerned about. (*Teachings of Harold B. Lee,* p. 49.)

Not only is it important to return home honorably, but a
husband and wife must do so as a couple. Exaltation is not ob-
tainable alone. The highest degree of glory requires that one
have a spouse of the opposite sex, one who is also worthy of the
highest honor God bestows on his children. Unfortunately, not
everyone will marry or be able to have children during mortality,
and that opportunity will have to come at a later time for many,
either in the spirit world, or during the Millennium. Those who
are single now, or who are in marriages that do not meet celestial
standards because of a spouse's obstinacy, will yet be exalted if
they honor baptismal and temple covenants. The Church organization ministers to both marrieds and singles. President Howard
W. Hunter gave this comforting counsel to those not yet married, or who live in difficult marriages:

> This is the church of Jesus Christ, not the church of marrieds
> or singles or any other group or individual. The gospel we preach
> is the gospel of Jesus Christ, which encompasses all the saving
> ordinances and covenants necessary to save and exalt every indi-
> vidual who is willing to accept Christ and keep the command-
> ments that he and our Father in Heaven have given. . . .
> May I hasten to add that no blessing, including that of eter-
> nal marriage and an eternal family, will be denied to any worthy
> individual. While it may take somewhat longer—perhaps even
> beyond this mortal life—for some to achieve this blessing, it will
> not be denied." (Howard W. Hunter, *Ensign,* June 1989, p. 76.)

Those who do not marry in this life, or who were married to
an unfaithful partner but have themselves been faithful, have not
forfeited marriage and family privileges.[17] Elder Dallin H. Oaks
taught that "through the merciful plan of our Father in Heaven,
persons who desire to do what is right but through no fault of

their own are unable to have an eternal marriage in mortal life will have an opportunity to qualify for eternal life in a period following mortality"—and here is the point—"if they keep the commandments of God and are true to their baptismal and other covenants." (Dallin H. Oaks, *Ensign*, October 1995, pp. 7–8.)

Our Father will give us every opportunity to succeed. For example, after baptism the person receives the gift of the Holy Ghost, a member of the Godhead, who is to be a revelator as necessary. God has established the Church with Apostles and prophets to explain and counsel us in the game plan of mortality. The day the Church was organized, the Lord gave Joseph Smith the calling to be "a seer, a translator, a prophet, an apostle of Jesus Christ." Church members were commanded to "give heed unto all [the Prophet's] words and commandments which he shall give unto you as he receiveth them, walking in all holiness before me; for his word ye shall receive, as if from mine own mouth, in all patience and faith. . . . For by doing these things the gates of hell shall not prevail against you; yea, and the Lord God will disperse the powers of darkness from before you, and cause the heavens to shake for your good, and his name's glory." (D&C 21:1, 4–6.) With priesthood leadership and counsel from the Lord's anointed in place, we are not left alone in our mortal tests even when they become severe. It is from prophets and Apostles and our own gift of the Holy Ghost that we learn to apply gospel principles to our family relationships. Ideas and inspiration on how to improve as marriage partners and parents are constant.

Hear their wisdom on the importance of marriage and family.

President Gordon B. Hinckley: "The most important step you have made or will make in your life is marriage. Its consequences are many, so important and so everlasting. No other decision will have such tremendous consequences for the future. Look to the establishment of a home in which there will be peace and happiness and love. Welcome the children who will come to that home, and rear them in the nurture and admonition of the Lord." (BYU commencement, Marriott Center, April 27, 1995, *Church News*, September 30, 1995, p. 2.)

President Howard W. Hunter: "The family is the most important unit in time and in eternity and, as such, transcends every other interest in life" (*Ensign,* November, 1994, p. 50).

President Ezra Taft Benson: "No other institution can take the place of the home or fulfill its essential function" ("The Values by Which to Live," *Leaders Magazine,* October-November 1984, p. 154).

Spencer W. Kimball: "Our success, individually and as a church, will largely be determined by how faithfully we focus on living the gospel in the home" (*Ensign,* May 1979, p. 83).

President Harold B. Lee: "The most important of the Lord's work you and I will ever do will be within the walls of our own homes." (*Stand Ye in Holy Places* [Salt Lake City: Deseret Book, 1974], p. 255.)

President Joseph Fielding Smith: "Marriage . . . is the foundation for eternal exaltation, for without it there could be no eternal progress in the kingdom of God. . . . There is no ordinance connected with the gospel of Jesus Christ of greater importance, of more solemn and sacred nature, and more necessary to the eternal joy of man, than marriage." (*Doctrines of Salvation,* Bruce R. McConkie, comp., Bookcraft, 1955, 2:58.)

President David O. McKay: "No other success can compensate for failure in the home" (*Improvement Era,* June 1964, p. 445).

In 1995, the First Presidency and Quorum of Twelve issued a proclamation on the family. It is only the second in the twentieth century and only the fifth since the Church's inception. I repeat it here as a worthwhile review and inspired resource.

THE FAMILY
A PROCLAMATION TO THE WORLD

We the First Presidency and the Council of the Twelve Apostles of The Church of Jesus Christ of Latter-day Saints, solemnly proclaim that marriage between a man and a woman is ordained of God and that the family is central to the Creator's plan for the eternal destiny of His children.

All human beings—male and female—are created in the image of God. Each is a beloved spirit son or daughter of heavenly parents, and, as such, each has a divine nature and destiny. Gender is an essential characteristic of individual premortal, mortal, and eternal identity and purpose.

In the premortal realm, spirit sons and daughters knew and worshiped God as their Eternal Father and accepted His plan by which His children could obtain a physical body and gain earthly experience to progress toward perfection and ultimately realize his or her divine destiny as an heir of eternal life. The divine plan of happiness enables family relationships to be perpetuated beyond the grave. Sacred ordinances and covenants available in holy temples make it possible for individuals to return to the presence of God and for families to be united eternally.

The first commandment that God gave to Adam and Eve pertained to their potential for parenthood as husband and wife. We declare that God's commandment for His children to multiply and replenish the Earth remains in force. We further declare that God has commanded that the sacred powers of procreation are to be employed only between man and woman, lawfully wedded as husband and wife.

We declare the means by which mortal life is created to be divinely appointed. We affirm the sanctity of life and of its importance in God's eternal plan.

Husband and wife have a solemn responsibility to love and care for each other and for their children. "Children are an heritage of the Lord" (Psalms 127:3). Parents have a sacred duty to rear their children in love and righteousness, to provide for their physical and spiritual needs, to teach them to love and serve one another, to observe the commandments of God and to be law-abiding citizens wherever they live. Husbands and wives—mothers and fathers—will be held accountable before God for the discharge of these obligations.

The family is ordained of God. Marriage between a man and woman is essential to His eternal plan. Children are entitled to birth within the bonds of matrimony, and to be reared by a father and a mother who honor marital vows with complete fidelity. Happiness in family life is most likely to be achieved

when founded upon the teachings of the Lord Jesus Christ.
Successful marriages and families are established and maintained
on principles of faith, prayer, repentance, forgiveness, respect,
love, compassion, work and wholesome recreational activities.
By divine design, fathers are to preside over their families in
love and righteousness and are responsible to provide the neces-
sities of life and the protection of their families. Mothers are primarily responsible for the nurture of their children. In these sacred responsibilities, fathers and mothers are obligated to help
one another as equal partners. Disability, death or other circumstances may necessitate individual adaptation. Extended families
should lend support when needed.

We warn that individuals who violate covenants of chastity,
who abuse spouse or offspring, or who fail to fulfill family responsibilities will one day stand accountable before God. Further, we warn that the disintegration of the family will bring
upon the individuals, communities and nations the calamities
foretold by ancient and modern prophets.

We call upon responsible citizens and officers of government
everywhere to promote those measures designed to maintain
and strengthen the family as the fundamental unit of society.
(*Ensign*, November 1995, p. 101.)

I submit that the nine keys suggested—faith, prayer, repentance, forgiveness, respect, love, compassion, work, wholesome
recreational activities—will strengthen and solidify family relations in ways that could work miracles if we would apply them
now in our family relations.

5

Exaltation

Perspective Five: Exaltation means living as God lives, in the family unit.

What do resurrected couples do? President Boyd K. Packer taught: "The ultimate purpose of all we teach is to unite parents and children in faith in the Lord Jesus Christ, that they are happy at home, sealed in an eternal marriage, linked to their generations, and assured of exaltation in the presence of our Heavenly Father" (*Ensign,* May 1995, p. 8).

Couples sealed in marriage will remain married in the spirit world and into eternity. Death only separates us for a brief time at the death of the first companion. As soon as we join each other in the spirit world, however, we are restored together as a married couple, for death does not affect the validity of our sealing; dying simply separates us until we meet again in the world of spirits. Elder Bruce R. McConkie taught this wonderful truth: "We have the power to perform a marriage, and we can do it so that the man and the woman become husband and wife here and now and—if they keep the covenant there and then made—they will remain husband and wife in the spirit world and will come up in glory and dominion with kingdoms and exaltation in the resurrection, being husband and wife and having eternal life. . . . That is our potential; that is within our possible realm of achievement." ("Celestial Marriage," *1977 Devotional Speeches of the Year,* p. 172.)

After death, though we live as married couples, we do not procreate, for spirits do not have that ability (otherwise Satan would be able to reproduce). The blessing of eternal increase will not be given us again until the morning of the first resurrection. The First Presidency explained:

> So far as the stages of eternal progression and attainment have been made known through divine revelation, we are to understand that only resurrected and glorified beings can become parents of spirit offspring. Only such exalted souls have reached maturity in the appointed course of eternal life; and the spirits born to them in the eternal worlds will pass in due sequence through the several stages or estates by which the glorified parents have attained exaltation. (First Presidency, 30 June 1916, in James R. Clark, ed., *Messages of the First Presidency,* Bookcraft, 1971 5:34.)

The term "eternal increase" means that as resurrected beings we are incapable of death and thus can have "an innumerable" posterity in eternity. Elder Melvin J. Ballard explained this concept of spirit children:

> What do we mean by endless or eternal increase? We mean that through the righteousness and faithfulness of men and women who keep the commandments of God they will come forth with celestial bodies, fitted and prepared to enter into their great, high and eternal glory in the celestial kingdom of God, and unto them, through their preparation, there will come spirit children. I don't think that is very difficult to comprehend. The nature of the offspring is determined by the nature of the substance that flows in the veins of the being. When blood flows in the veins of the being the offspring will be what blood produces, which is tangible flesh and bone; but when that which flows in the veins is spirit matter, a substance which is more refined and pure and glorious than blood, the offspring of such beings will be spirit children. (Melvin J. Ballard, "The Three Degrees of Glory," Ogden Tabernacle, September 22, 1922; Deseret Book, pamphlet, p. 10.)

How obvious this turns out to be when you consider the wisdom of our Father! Why institute a plan of salvation if it is only temporary? Why would we leave our premortal home and come to a mortal probation if we were simply to die and pass out of existence? If the Savior's mission was not to save husbands and wives and children as a family unit, then what *is* the purpose of the gospel plan and its centerpiece, the Atonement? "To forgive sins," many would answer. And that is an important aspect of the Atonement, because we make so many mistakes as mortals. But there is so much more involved in the mission and suffering of Jesus Christ than simply clearing mistakes. After repenting and being cleansed, then what? The Latter-day Saint religion is just practical enough to raise this question: "What do resurrected beings do if they are no longer subject to death?"

The answer, of course, turns out to be a continuation of married couples and family members. Eternity is simply a continuation of earth life where we possess bodies that do not decay or die. Consider that there are two times in eternity when we are able to bear children: (1) during a period of mortality when we possess a physical body of element combined with our spirit body, and (2) as resurrected beings when again the physical body will be combined with the spirit.[18] Thus the Savior's offerings as our Redeemer, our Resurrector, the Restorer of Marriage and Family Relations, are his most important contributions to us! How grateful married lovers ought to be for that aspect of his mortal mission! The kingdom of heaven is designed for married couples who cherish each other and want their marriage and family relationships to be everlasting and who live according to the principles that will lead to that end.[19]

As children of God, we live from eternity to eternity. This means that we live from a premortal eternity to a post-resurrection eternity. Consider the following diagram:

Temple Marriage

Premortal Eternity ----▶ Mortality ------------------▶ Postmortal Eternity
(premortal life   We marry and become   The Atonement
with Father)   parents for the first time   makes possible an
                                               eternal marriage and
                                               eternal increase

The meaning of eternity can best be understood if it is split by a temple marriage. The continuum above shows the eternity of the premortal life on the left and the eternity of the post-resurrection on the right. Up until the time when we are sealed by priesthood authority during mortality, we have been single for a long premortal and a brief mortal period. Following marriage, if we keep the covenants we make in the temple, we will never be separated again in all eternity except for the short period between the death of one spouse and the time they meet again in the spirit world. Thus a temple marriage not only becomes the crowning ordinance of the gospel of Jesus Christ but also an important division between the period of singleness and our being eternal companions as exalted beings.

THE NEED FOR TEMPLE WORK

It has been the relentless work of Satan to destroy our Father's plan of marriage and family and unfortunately he has been only too successful. Almost all of those who were our brothers and sisters in the premortal life did not live in mortality at a time and place when priesthood power and keys were available and thus when couples could be sealed in marriage by priesthood ordinance. Ordinance work for the dead is one of the major efforts of the Church in this last dispensation. How could those who lived at an earlier time enjoy the blessings that are available to us in these latter days without research to identify them and allow them the same privileges as we enjoy? Those whose records have been lost or are otherwise unavailable will come back at the beginning of the Millennium to provide us with the records presently unavailable. "The Lord has said through his servants," said Elder Joseph Fielding Smith, "that during the millennium those who have passed beyond and have attained the resurrection will reveal in person to those who are still in mortality all the information which is required to complete the work of these who have passed from this life. Then the dead will have the privilege of making known the things they desire and are entitled to receive. In this way no soul will be neglected and the work of the Lord will be perfected." (*Doctrines of Salvation,* 3:65.)

Even though most people today believe and hope that love and marriage are eternal (as witnessed by song lyrics, personal marriage vows, and religious surveys), this concept is not a part of extant theologies. Satan has labored long and hard to convince people that no such doctrine exists.[20] As President Boyd K. Packer taught: "The adversary is jealous toward all who have the power to beget life. He cannot beget life; he is impotent" (*Ensign,* May 1992, p. 66). He knows that through the atonement of Jesus Christ everyone has the potential of keeping their families intact throughout all eternity.

This concept of marriage and family as taught by the Latter-day Saints has been soundly ridiculed by many Christians who claim belief in the redemptive mission of Jesus Christ.[21] As Church members our attitude is: "If marriage does not last forever, what is the purpose of marriage? Why were Adam and Eve commanded to have children? What does redemption really mean? When it is clear from the scriptures that we are resurrected with flesh and bone bodies, why would anyone simply want to sing in a choir or fill the universe as an unembodied spirit forever when our potential as sons and daughters of God is much more profound?! It is one of the most ironic twists that Satan has convinced people that marriage is a temporary phenomenon, in effect the worst possible denial of the Atonement of the Lord Jesus Christ.

Thus the gospel plan resolves our worst fear—being separate and alone throughout all eternity. And this possibility of marriage beyond death provides reasons to bridle mortal passions and becomes an incentive to live righteously.

How would a man or woman treat a spouse or child who they know can be part of their eternal family? It is not ordinances alone that save us. Salvation requires that each of us must live worthy lives. Elder Robert D. Hales explained that "an eternal bond doesn't just happen as a result of sealing covenants we make in the temple. How we conduct ourselves in this life will

determine what we will be in all the eternities to come. To receive the blessings of the sealing that our Heavenly Father has
given to us, we have to keep the commandments and conduct
ourselves in such a way that our families will want to live with us
in the eternities" (*Ensign,* November, 1996, p. 65).

If we are unworthy of exaltation, then we are kidding ourselves about eternal family relationships. If we treat our loved
ones shabbily, manifest temperamental behavior, demonstrate
little love or affection, show no interest in their needs, why
would they want to live with us forever, since we have not been
much to live with here? Assuming the ordinances have been received, what we have done with our agency will be most important in the day of judgment. Exaltation is possible only if the
quality of our relationships with each other are such that family
members want to be together, not because of magic words in an
ordinance. God would not force a righteous wife to be sealed to
a wicked husband or vice versa. Children will not be sealed to
unworthy parents. The more Christlike we become as individuals, the more lovable and attractive we become and the more
one's spouse and children will be honored to be members of
one's family. The corollary to this is that the more like Satan we
were to become, the less attractive or desirable our company
would be. No one would choose to be around us, and we would
not be fit beings for heaven. Thus every Latter-day Saint who
understands the mission of Jesus Christ and loves his or her family will desire to live so as to merit the blessings of being together for an unlimited duration.

President David O. McKay tied behavior to our feelings and
beliefs in the Son of God in this way: "What you sincerely in
your heart think of Christ will determine what you are, will
largely determine what your acts will be." ("Gospel Ideals,"
Improvement Era, 1953, p. 34.)

6

Problems and Gospel Principles

Perspective Six: Marriage and family problems develop because we fail to apply the principles of the gospel.

As Latter-day Saints it is easy for us to idealize marriage and family life, for we have been taught from the cradle up that marriage in the temple—marriage for eternity—is the only way to marry if we expect to be happy. We believe, and rightly so, that marriage will be the most intimate and important relationship we form with another human being in mortality. We believe marriage to be preferable to remaining single. Thus, before we marry, we anticipate being married. We picture ourselves beautifully outfitted in the holy temple.

Following the ceremony, reception, and honeymoon, we expect to settle in our first apartment. We see ourselves affectionately kissing each other good-by as we separate for our day's labor, and returning home from work, happy to be back together. We will enjoy a humble meal together, share the events of the day, exchange profound insights, read verses of scripture together, exchange exquisite back and foot rubs, and so on. It sounds so simple. What a grand view we develop of this marriage business before we get to the altar!

But ideals often get in the way of reality. President Spencer W. Kimball reminded us:

Two people coming from different backgrounds soon learn after the ceremony is performed that stark reality must be faced. There is no longer a life of fantasy or of make-believe; we must come out of the clouds and put our feet firmly on the earth.

Responsibility must be assumed and new duties must be accepted. Some personal freedoms must be relinquished, and many adjustments, unselfish adjustments, must be made.

One comes to realize very soon after the marriage that the spouse has weaknesses not previously revealed or discovered. The virtues that were constantly magnified during courtship now grow relatively smaller, and the weaknesses that seemed so small and insignificant during courtship now grow to sizable proportions. The hour has come for understanding hearts, for self-appraisal, and for good common sense, reasoning, and planning. ("Marriage and Divorce," BYU Devotional, September 7, 1976, p. 4.)

Elder Marlin K. Jensen gave this (probably) typical experience he and his wife had early in their marriage:

We were living in Salt Lake City, where I was attending law school and Kathy was teaching first grade. Under the stress of being new to the city, our respective schools, and each other, our relationship became a bit testy. One night at about dinnertime, we had a quarrel that convinced me that I need not hope for nourishment at home. So I left our modest apartment and walked to the nearest fast-food restaurant, a block away.

As I entered the north door of the establishment, I looked to my right—and much to my surprise, I saw Kathy entering through the south door! We exchanged angry glances and advanced to opposing cash registers to place our orders. We continued to ignore each other as we sat alone on opposite ends of the restaurant, sullenly eating our evening meals. We then left as we had entered and took our separate routes home. It wasn't until later that we reconciled and laughed together about how infantile we had been. (*Ensign,* October 1994, p. 47.)

Marriage has a way of testing us in every personality and character attribute we thought we had mastered before marriage.

As we mature in spirituality and common sense through the experiences of married life, we come to realize, as did the Jensens, that as newly marrieds we all (1) have unrealistic expectations as to the course marriage will take; (2) hide some of the real us during our dating and courtship days (as did our partner); (3) have the belief that temple marriages are automatically guarantors of peace and tranquility; and (4) think we can resolve any marital problem that might surface as long as we can sleep together. We never expect *major* problems to disrupt the serenity of our married life. Maybe toothpaste caps would be left off, or the bathroom tissue might roll the wrong way, but minor differences would be quickly resolved by rational discourse.

We soon learn that the realities of marriage throw us. So can parenthood. Somehow we are, when it comes right down to it, never quite prepared for the experiences marriage brings. Recall President Gordon B. Hinckley's concern: "We have wonderful people, but we have too many whose families are falling apart. It is a matter of serious concern; I think it is my most serious concern. I wish to see our people walk in the light of the Lord." (*Church News,* June 7, 1995.)

I think Carlfred Broderick's analysis of why divorces among the Saints are on the increase despite our understanding of the gospel is meaningful here:

> Often I have asked myself why [our divorce rate is increasing.] Latter-day Saints know the principles of eternal unity. I am persuaded that there is no principle of successful marital life that I could share with good LDS couples that would be new to them. In fact, any principle that purported to be true and crucial to successful living which was new to them should be immediately suspect. The laws governing marital satisfaction are but special applications of the laws of the gospel, and every good Latter-day Saint learned them in Primary (or, in the case of converts, in the six missionary discussions and the Gospel Principles classes on Sundays).

He then gave an illustration of how we fail to grasp the power of gospel principles to solve our dilemmas:

The point was illustrated vividly in an experience with a colleague. He is Jewish and one of the finest family therapists I know. I have referred close friends and relatives to him with good results. One day a woman called me to see if she could make an appointment to bring in her family for some counseling. Their problem was a rebellious teenager and an escalating power struggle between the girl and her parents that was getting out of hand. . . .

. . . After only a couple of weeks I got a call from my friend. "Carl, I need some help with this couple you referred to me."

"What's the problem? They probably just need to loosen up the parental iron fist a little."

"Of course. If they don't, this kid is about to run away from home or attempt suicide or do something else drastic. But, Carl, every time I suggest any movement in the direction of loosening up they patiently explain to me that I just don't understand their religious obligations as Mormon parents to keep this kid in line. Frankly, I don't know how to deal with this. I don't want to attack their religious beliefs, but the situation is explosive."

I thought a moment and then said, "Here's what you do. First, tell them that since you have started working with them on their problems you have developed a real curiosity about the Mormon religion. . . . Then say that there is one issue that keeps coming up when you ask about it that has you mystified. You keep hearing about some 'war in heaven,' but you can never quite figure out what it is about."

"That's it? I just ask them to explain this 'war in heaven'"?

"That's it."

"Carl, what's the war in heaven?"

"It doesn't matter; just do what I said, and let me know how it goes."

A few days later he called: "Carl, I can't believe it. I did what you said and it was like magic."

"So tell me about the session."

"Well, as you suggested, I told them that since I started working with them I had become sort of interested in the Mormon religion. You wouldn't believe the response. Even the rebellious teenage kid promised to give me a copy of some book on the Church with the family picture in the front. Then I said, there was just one thing that kind of confused me about their beliefs. I kept hearing about some war in heaven. What was this war in heaven? Well, the mom in this family didn't as much as take a minute to collect her thoughts. In seconds she had launched into some story about a council in heaven and two plans, and she gets about three minutes into it and she stops cold in her tracks and gives me a funny look and says, "All right, Doctor, you've made your point." From that point on they were like putty in my hands. It was like magic, Carl, what is this war in heaven?" (In *Eternal Companions,* Bookcraft, 1995, pp. 10–12.)

Sometimes I wonder if we are so used to meetings, firesides, conferences, scriptural recitations and quotations given in Church meetings that we think "we know it all already," or "we have heard that before," without allowing these passages and messages to stop in the middle of our gray matter. In a class that I have taught on "living prophets," at both the Institute and BYU, we study general conference talks. My students and I have learned, over the years, that when you read conference talks in their printed form they are much more powerful, inspirational, and lasting than when we simply listen or view them on television.

During our viewing the phone rings or we become distracted; or we become drowsy after a meal in the afternoon, and often we miss major parts of the messages. We fail to appreciate what we missed because we thought we got the "general drift," anyway, and it sounded familiar, like all the other talks we have heard over the years. My students have been greatly surprised at how much material passed by them in contrast to the experience of reading and underlining. It reminds me of a statement by President Spencer W. Kimball concerning the scriptures:

I ask us all to honestly evaluate our performance in scripture study. It is a common thing to have a few passages of scripture at our disposal, floating in our minds, as it were, and thus to have the illusion that we know a great deal about the gospel. In this sense, having a little knowledge can be a problem indeed. I am convinced that each of us, at some time in our lives, must discover the scriptures for ourselves—and not just discover them once, but rediscover them again and again. (*Ensign,* September 1976, p. 3.)

Our difficulty is in making the connection between gospel principles and behavioral practices. Let me share what I consider the most important scripture that strengthens marriages, because it provides the very key to successful families. It is easy to miss if we are not careful because it requires that we make the connection to our family life. The scripture is in 4 Nephi, and the account follows the Lord's visit to the Nephites on the American continent. Let's look carefully at this passage:

> And it came to pass in the thirty and sixth year, the people were all converted unto the Lord, upon all the face of the land . . . and there were no contentions and disputations among them, and every man did deal justly one with another.

We find all the Nephites and Lamanites at peace with each other and all of them were converted to the gospel of Jesus Christ.

> And now, behold, it came to pass that the people of Nephi did wax strong, and did multiply exceedingly fast, and became an exceedingly fair and delightsome people.

When you multiply exceedingly fast, that is faster than normal. Here we learn that righteous people look forward to having children; unrighteous people find them a nuisance, an expense, and for them certainly a large family would not be desirable.

> And it came to pass that there was *no contention* in the land because of the love of God which did dwell in the hearts of the people.

Now we find out that the reason for the tranquility and lack of contention is what Mormon called the "love of God" in the hearts of each person. Now look at the result of their having this love in their hearts:

> And there were no envyings, nor strifes, nor tumults, nor whoredoms, nor lyings, nor murders, nor any manner of lasciviousness, and surely there could not be a happier people among all the people who had been created by the hand of God.
>
> There were no robbers, nor murderers . . . they were in one, the children of Christ, and heirs to the kingdom of God.
>
> And how blessed were they! For the Lord did bless them in all their doings; yea, even they were blessed and prospered until an hundred and ten years had passed away; . . . and there was no contention in all the land. (4 Nephi 1:2, 10, 15–18; emphasis added.)

The most wonderful, peaceful period in Nephite history began as these people had acquired the "love of God" in their hearts. These Nephite Saints were able to live for more than two hundred years without contention or bloodshed. Can you imagine: two centuries of peace and no fighting, quarreling, or killing after they had been mortal enemies? If we could understand what is meant by the "love of God," I think we also could understand how we could do the same thing in our relationships, our homes, wards, stakes, and the Church, and the communities around us. Let us consider what this scripture means. Perhaps then we can duplicate among us the Nephites' behavior.

When the Savior appeared to the righteous Saints gathered at the temple in Bountiful they saw him descend from heaven. They heard him speak, and soon each one came forward to touch him, to speak with him. That opportunity taught the Nephites some basic gospel doctrines rather quickly and in a profound way that changed their lives for good. Consider what doctrines they now clearly understood:

—Resurrected beings have tangible bodies

—Resurrected beings look like mortals (see also D&C 129:7–8; the only reason we want to touch a visitor is to discern the nature of the body, because mortals and immortals look alike; you can't tell the difference between mortals and immortals just by looking with your natural eyes).

—Resurrected beings converse, socialize, and live the gospel as they do in mortality. Death does not really change our nature, our gender, or our feelings for each other.

What does this have to do with marriage? Everything! Consider what doctrine a Nephite couple would now know and understand, doctrine that did not come from reading books or hearing sermons. I imagine a husband, after that personal visit at Bountiful with the Savior, saying to his wife: "Dear, do you realize what we just did. That person over there who we just visited with and embraced, and we felt the prints in his hands and feet, is the Son of God! He is Jesus Christ, the same one who was born and ministered among the Jews only to be killed by their leaders. Yet he is now resurrected.

Do you realize what that means to you and me? It means that even though you and I are aging and will someday die, we will be resurrected just as he now is. That is his gift to us. And then we will continue as male and female and can continue as husband and wife, for once we are resurrected we can never die again; and that makes it possible for us to be eternal companions! And our children are going through the same life cycle as we are and will also come forth as resurrected beings someday. That enables us to be an eternal family if we will simply do as he taught us."

Wow! Can you see how an understanding of the mission of Jesus Christ provides a resurrected body for each of us, allowing us to be both immortal and yet still married? How wonderful the atonement of Jesus Christ is in what it does for married couples who love each other and their children with a love that does not cease at death!

To appreciate the privilege of being together eternally would give you such an outpouring of love for Jesus Christ for what he has done for the two of you (assuming you love your spouse and children and want to be together forever). Would not your heart be overflowing with love and appreciation for the very Being who made an everlasting relationship possible? Would not your heart be filled too with the "love of God," as it was with this group of Nephites?[22] Their experience was so powerful that the effects of this doctrinal realization enabled them to carry on as a righteous people for over ten decades. It was not until later generations that those who did not personally experience this event fell into apostasy. (See 4 Nephi 1:22–26; Mosiah 26:1–4.)

Once the doctrine of the resurrection and eternal marriage becomes a reality in our minds and hearts, who would want to live in a world of fighting and bickering? It would be a form of insanity to treat each other with less than the utmost care and consideration. (Can you imagine our heavenly parents arguing? Or members of the Godhead being sarcastic with each other?)

Jesus brought immortality and eternal life to fallen men and women, and that concept was so clear to these individuals at Bountiful that it changed and softened their hearts toward each other and their children. With the "love of God" ingrained into their souls, they now understood their full potential—the possibility of living forever as companions and family. They could see that their children would follow the same life cycle and could become part of their eternal family unit, and therefore they would treat them with great kindness, the type of kindness we all use when we are dating or trying to impress one another.

RESOLVING MARITAL CONFLICT: POWER FROM A SCRIPTURAL EXAMPLE

The only example of a serious marital argument being resolved in the scriptures comes from a Book of Mormon account of Lehi and Sariah. Sariah became discouraged at the prospect that her sons were dead and would not return from their trip to Jerusalem to secure the brass plates. She complained to her husband, making serious personal charges. This experience could have fractured their relationship had they been lesser people, but Lehi was true to his covenants and to his appreciation for his wife. He responded to his wife's concerns in a Christlike way.

Let's look more closely at this account of how a prophet and his wife resolved a major marital disagreement. Her concerns were not minor issues. We are not talking about toothpaste/toilet seat up or down/toilet paper roll direction here. We are talking about huge threats to a marriage relationship.

After the family had left everything at their Jerusalem residence and gone off into the wilderness, Nephi and his brothers were sent back to obtain the plates of brass. Sariah became concerned about the safety of her children when they were late in returning. (Nephi and his brothers were delayed in obtaining the record, having to devise several stratagems to secure the record from Laban, but Sariah did not have a phone or a fax machine by which to know that.) Mom began to think that her sons must have been killed and the entire family was now in great danger. She assumed the worst—not unlike most of us when something does not go our way or we reason out of fear.

Sariah knew of the dangerous conditions that prevailed in Jerusalem, for the Jews had tried to kill her husband. Remember that Laban was carrying a sword at the time Nephi found him, indicating the insecurity that existed in the city.

She had every reason to be worried about her sons. She reasoned to herself that there was a good chance they had been captured and killed, and they therefore would not come back at all. If the boys were recognized in Jerusalem as part of Lehi's family, perhaps they would be detained or thrown into prison, a fate already suffered by Jeremiah (see 1 Nephi 7:14). She could imagine all sorts of scenarios—all of them negative. It is a trait of mothers. But what conscientious mother could not identify with the fears that welled up inside Sariah. And who was responsible for their present predicament? Who had sent the boys back to the big city?

So we see what she was thinking when she voiced four major complaints against Lehi:

1. She accused Lehi of being a "visionary man"—perhaps meaning that he had moved his family out of their comfortable home at Jerusalem because of visions he claimed to have seen (which she apparently had not seen), and now the family was liv-

ing in a precarious and hostile environment. Their own lives were now threatened.

2. The family estate was gone. The family left practically everything they owned in order to escape Jewish threats of death. Lehi had been a good provider, as evidenced by the treasures the sons brought to Laban in an effort to exchange their wealth for the plates. Laban's avarice caused him to covet their possessions, and he wanted them killed so as to obtain their riches. Had there not been an impressive array of treasure he would not have tried to kill them to obtain it.

3. It was not improbable to think that the boys were already dead, for they were gone longer than she knew the trip should take.

4. If her sons did not return, then she and Lehi too would undoubtedly die in the wilderness; if not from lack of food, from bands of marauders and thieves (they could build no fires, as that might attract attention).

When we read this account from our easy chairs of the twenty-first century we may be quick to criticize Sariah. If you have done much camping, however, you realize how quickly things can turn around (my fishing line gets snagged, mosquitoes are trying to carry us away, flies are all over our meals, clothes are dirty, sleeping bags are inadequate and feel suffocating, air mattresses go flat at 2:00 A.M.) A journey that may have seemed like a good idea at the time they left the Jerusalem area could turn into a disaster. Camping for a few days may sound wonderful; for this family, however, it would go on for eight years, and Sariah would bear two sons in the wilderness away from family and friends and help. Given these considerations, leaving home for good doesn't sound very appealing. Realizing the situation this family found themselves in, most of us would have sided with Sariah. Try putting yourself in her place and realize how difficult it was for her to understand why things were not working out for them if this was the Lord's will in the first place. (You and I may fall to pieces over much less.)

Even if Lehi's former home didn't have a new automobile sitting in the garage, or a giant TV screen in the front room, with running water, toilets, shirts and pants that don't wrinkle, and sunscreen for the desert sun, his family no doubt had more than the usual comforts of the day. Imagine what the family gave up to follow their father into a dangerous wilderness. Now Sariah was discouraged, and she questioned the wisdom of her husband's leadership. She was becoming more impatient and worried as each day passed with no word from her children.

Lehi, however, like all prophets, was a prototype of Christ. If you think about it, we have no accounts that would suggest how Jesus might have handled this challenge. Obviously we have no record of Jesus being married and dealing with what we consider normal adjustments to marriage, or of having, for example, a two-year-old or a teenager to disturb the serenity of life. But since the Savior was perfect in every area, we are confident he would have handled to perfection any family situation arising from another person's imperfections or immaturity.

In Lehi we have a chance to see in some detail what a Christ-like personality—one who had been on the mount, so to speak, one who had close contact with the heavens, as witnessed by visions and revelations—would do in these circumstances. How would a god handle a discouraged and frustrated wife? True to his calling as a prophet, a husband, a father, Lehi comes through as a man of God. It is worthwhile to see how he responded to his wife following her personal attack on his leadership, his "inspiration," about how, where, and why he was leading the family into this desert adventure.

He addressed each of her four concerns directly, kindly, humbly, and charitably. To her first concern about being a visionary man, the essential reason why they were in the wilderness, he explained: [Dear], "I know that I am a visionary man; for if I had not seen the things of God in a vision I should not have known the goodness of God, but had tarried at Jerusalem, and had perished with my brethren" (1 Nephi 5:4).

Notice that here there was no attacking of Sariah's family background, or of weaknesses she may have had in the past, no accusing her of being disloyal to priesthood leadership. There was no temper tantrum or threatening to sleep outside the tent.

In effect he simply and humbly said: "Sweetheart, you have a good point. I can see that you are concerned and I don't blame you for feeling the way you do. I can only tell you what I know and what I have experienced; and I want you to know that I am sure of my inspiration. In fact, I've never been more sure of anything in my life. The Lord has shown me what would have happened had we remained at Jerusalem, and it is not pretty. I would not have believed it myself if the Lord had not been kind enough to show it all to me in vision. Please be patient and let's trust the Lord."

Her second objection partly concerned the loss of their family home and estate, their comforts, resources, wealth and possessions. Lehi responded to her concern with: "I know that we have lost everything of a material nature. Our consolation is that we are gaining a land of promise, a land that has everything we could possibly want. I rejoice in that knowledge and know that you will also. We may have lost our old land and home, but we are going to a place that will more than compensate us for what we have lost.

"We will be the only ones to occupy this new land, and it is teeming with resources that will allow us to rebuild what we have lost. It will be a great blessing to our family if we can only hold out until we get there. I know that doesn't sound too helpful right now, and we have some tough days ahead of us. It has not been nor will it be easy for any of us. But we have the Lord's promises on which to rely. We have an important mission that the Lord has asked of us and he will compensate us well for the loss of our property and home."

To her third objection—our sons will be killed if they are not already dead—he said, "I know that the Lord will deliver [our] sons out of the hands of Laban, and bring them down again unto us in the wilderness" (1 Nephi 5:5). You can almost hear Lehi say, "Yes, honey, I know it is a dangerous trip. But it was the Lord who asked this of them and I know that the Lord will inspire them and protect them and they will return unharmed."

Her last concern, that they themselves would be killed, was answered in his reply that the boys would return safely and then their family would continue their journey until they reached the land of promise.

How do we know that Lehi answered her in this manner? After all, we are getting this entire story through Nephi's pen. Perhaps he removed the emotion from the account by the time he wrote it years later. Answer: Because the account says: "And after this manner of language did my father, Lehi, comfort my mother, Sariah, concerning us" (1 Nephi 5:6). In other words, Sariah's concerns, to use a missionary phrase, were resolved. She was still apprehensive until her sons returned, but he had comforted her. I think we can take that to mean that by his answering each of her fears she was assured by the Spirit of the Lord that everything would work out for both their sons and them.

No wonder Nephi records that his parents "did rejoice"; more specifically, Lehi "was filled with joy, and also my mother, Sariah, was exceedingly glad, for she truly had mourned because of us" (1 Nephi 5:1).

Nephi records that when the sons had safely returned, his parents' "joy was full, and my mother was comforted" (v. 7). It was such a complete relief and testimony-building experience for her that she bore witness of her husband's calling: "Now I know of a surety that the Lord hath commanded my husband to flee into the wilderness; yea, and I also know of a surety that the Lord hath protected my sons, and delivered them out of the hands of Laban, and given them power whereby they could accomplish the thing which the Lord hath commanded them" (1 Nephi 5:8).

After learning the details of the adventure to retrieve the plates of brass, Sariah was further assured of her husband's inspiration and she became again a willing companion, ready to endure whatever it took to accomplish their task.

In our latter-day softness, with thermostats and modern comforts, perhaps we can glide by all this because we know the outcome. But as often happens in life, men and women are soon tested after they profess their love for the Lord and are willing to follow Church leaders. (The Apostle Peter, soon after bearing testimony of Jesus Christ, comes to mind.) After we have had an experience that seems to firm up our testimony, it is as if Satan gets a crack at us to see if we will really keep the commitment we so recently made. If our hearts have been truly softened, if we are forgiven of our sins, if we rise above our fears, then we are able to face new trials without any baggage from the past. But if in our hearts we have not "gotten over it," have simply buried it, it may spring up again when the next test comes along.

Notice the character of Sariah, when only a short time later she too was forced to re-check her heart and testimony. From the record: "It came to pass that the Lord spake unto him [my father, not my mother; or not my parents] again, saying that it was not meet for him, Lehi, that he should take his family into the wilderness alone; but that his sons should take daughters to wife, that they might raise up seed unto the Lord in the land of promise" (1 Nephi 7:1). Can you not see a lesser woman saying, "Okay, look, once was enough. You lucked out the first time and the boys came back safely, but now I've had it. Didn't you hear how close they came to getting killed? Laban almost killed them. Did you forget that so soon? And you want them to go back into that environment? Laban's soldiers will be looking for his killers. What kind of nonsense is this, anyway?"

Yet in the record we get no such words from this wonderful and Christlike mother; not a word of complaint—ever again. She is thoroughly convinced that her husband knows what he is doing and she is willing to follow his counsel even if it means that her sons are going to take off and leave the couple alone in the wilderness again. Her conversion was so complete that Nephi says, after the sons' initial return, that "they did rejoice exceedingly, and did offer sacrifice and burnt offerings unto the Lord; and they gave thanks to the God of Israel" (1 Nephi 5:9).

No doubt Sariah was her husband's equal. Great men usually have great women to support them. It is a credit to her that so far as the record goes she never again wavered. And certainly her tests were not over. She had to cook food in primitive conditions. When the family ran out of food she held steady, even when her husband questioned his own inspiration. There is no indication of any complaint on her part. She experienced at least two pregnancies during the rough journey, saw two of her sons rebel against her husband and Nephi, and yet remained on the Lord's side through it all.

It says something about Lehi too: he was genuine; he was filled with the Spirit of the Lord and humble enough to help his wife through a difficult period, a period when he could have attacked her lack of faith, her family upbringing, and perhaps events from earlier days in their marriage, actions that perhaps many of us would have used to justify and retaliate. But he answered her concerns as best he could, and it resulted in her being "comforted" by his Christlike responses. What a wonderful example of resolving a major marital disagreement! What wife and mother, filled with the emotions and concerns of motherhood, does not question her husband's motives and his inspiration at some time or another?

Perhaps the next time we feel threatened or under attack, or feel that our spouse doesn't understand our motives, we need to recall the great example of a Christlike man, Lehi, and his character that allowed him to be a comfort to his family through his blessing them, his inspired direction, and his reminding them of the doctrines of the gospel along with the history of the Jews.

Perhaps we too can be an example to our children, as Lehi was to his. May we remember, as wives, that it is not easy to lead a family, to always know the reasons for our inspiration—until later. May we as husbands realize that our wives have different concerns sometimes than we do, that mothers worry about each one of their children while husbands may stay a little less emotionally concerned. May we support each other as wives and husbands; may we be compassionate as we contemplate various roles we carry out in marriage that require us to be men and women of Christ. May we be Latter-day Saints in the highest sense of the term. For perhaps, like Lehi and Sariah, even when we are at our best we may have children who stray.

7

Marriage Quality Determines Subsequent Family

Perspective Seven: As the marriage goes, so goes the family.

Knowing that marriage and family relationships can extend beyond this brief span of mortality, of course, does not mean that we are without challenges in our mortal married lives or in dealing with our children. This principle, however, should give us a perspective that influences us to work together, to cooperate, to build family relationships, and to view divorce as a last resort due to major sins such as infidelity and/or abuse. Our theological foundation provides the incentive to strive more diligently to be an effective companion and parent.

Latter-day Saints are in the marriage and family business! All mortals are. Each of us is born to a mother and father and we spend our early years under their tutelage. We grow up and eventually leave our folks to begin a family of our own. We bear children who then grow up only to do to us what we did much earlier to our own folks—leave home. We then become the older generation of grandparents and great-grandparents.

Marriage is a profound experience. We select one other individual from the vast number of spirits that have come to this earth. Often we come from completely different backgrounds. We invite another to join us in a lasting alliance, as this union makes us more complete. Alone we are not whole. Maintaining and enriching this coupling is of high priority.

Our decision to marry is of such importance that the Lord has us marry in "his house," to sanctify the marriage and make it permanent. It was an important part of the Redeemer's mission that we might be sealed together in this life and then rise in the resurrection with bodies capable of continuing our love and our desire to be together. Having married, we bring other spirit children from the premortal realm to join our family here, and we become their tutors and mentors as they repeat the same cycle as we have. They will forever be our children even though they grow up to become adults, marry, and become parents themselves. We are tied together in a patriarchal chain.

When you consider marriage and family in this eternal framework, the conclusion is obvious: What project could be more engaging, more rewarding, interesting, challenging, demanding, and yet worthwhile and worthy of our best efforts? In an important way we imitate the "work" of our heavenly parents by preparing our family for immortality and exaltation. Their success adds to our "glory" and satisfaction.

President Howard W. Hunter reminded husbands and fathers that "one of the greatest things a father can do for his children is to love their mother" (*Ensign,* November, 1994, p. 50). The corollary to this is, "One of the greatest things a mother can do for her children is to love their father." It could be said too that "one of the greatest things a father and mother can do for their children is to model a healthy marriage."

One of the old clichés of family relations is that "as the marriage goes, so goes the family." It is a husband and wife who establish the prototype of what subsequent families will look like and how they function. If the first model succeeds well, the likelihood increases that subsequent versions of that model will also do well, for the initial couple sets the tone for those that follow. President James E. Faust gave us this perspective:

> In my opinion, the teaching, rearing, and training of children requires more intelligence, intuitive understanding, humil-

ity, strength, wisdom, spirituality, perseverance, and hard work than any other challenge we might have in life. This is especially so when moral foundations of honor and decency are eroding around us. . . .

Generally, those children who make the decision and have the resolve to abstain from drugs, alcohol, and illicit sex are those who have adopted and internalized the strong values of their homes as lived by their parents. In times of difficult decisions they are most likely to follow the teachings of their parents rather than the example of their peers or the sophistries of the media which glamorize alcohol consumption, illicit sex, infidelity, dishonesty, and other vices. . . .

What seems to help cement parental teachings and values in place in children's lives is a firm belief in Deity" (James E. Faust, *Ensign*, November 1990, pp. 33–34).

Our task as married couples is to lead our family back to Heavenly Father. To do so, we must help our children to develop mental, physical, and emotional traits that will allow them to attract a mate of their own and establish their own family. Where parents manifest healthy personalities and a stable marriage, where they incorporate Christlike traits in their relationships with each other, their offspring have a greater chance to develop healthy psyches and establish sound principles of behavior in their own marriages. The cycle continues forever. Because every human being comes through two parents, it is through those headwaters that each person will either be contaminated or will, like the pure and unadulterated stream, flow onward and outward to accomplish its foreordained purpose.

HEALTHY MARRIAGE RELATIONSHIPS FOR PARENTS: THE KEY

The first principle of effective parenting is the mental and emotional health of individual parents and the quality of their alliance. Generally we can say that healthy parents produce healthy children. There are exceptions, of course. But if the marriage is adequate (it doesn't have to be perfect) and there is a clear demonstration of healthy male-female relationships on the part of the parents, the chances for normal, well-rounded children increase. Parents who love each other and demonstrate that love to their children have a head start in the critical elements of effective parenting. Children from spouses who love each other are more likely to be cherished by both parents, as the children are an extension of their conjugal love. Just as the genetic components of both parents are passed to their posterity, so children who feel loved by their parents are influenced by the model of their parents. When the marriage relationship is healthy, children are more inclined to adopt the values and standards of their parents.

THE IMPACT OF MARRIAGE ON CHILDREN

What specific impact does marriage have on children? I am convinced that most of us do not realize the importance that the quality of our union plays in the lives of our children, not only in developing their personalities but also in how each one views himself as a male or a female, how he or she approaches life in general, acquires relationship skills, and develops other traits and attributes that contribute to individual mental health and happiness. It is, after all, from the parental example (or lack of it) that children learn (or do not learn) to perform well the roles or script of marriage. Though siblings and peers will greatly influence the lives of children on the path to maturity, parents are normally the most important role models children see as to how their own marriages and interpersonal relationships should function.

Christlike traits of charity, kindness, love, long-suffering, meekness, gentleness, manners, affection, respect for gender similarities and differences, and decency between men and women are only the beginning of the lessons infused into the souls of children who have observed the behavior of loving parents. Modeling is still the best of teaching techniques (for good or ill). A strong marriage carries with it a greater likelihood that children will grow up with both the desire and the ability to attract a spiritual and emotional equal who is also equipped to consummate the marriage and to bear and rear impressive children. These offspring, in turn, replace the parents with well-rounded, healthy citizens. Though there are occasional exceptions, children who come from homes where parents love each other are generally better prepared to assume the demands of marriage.

COUNSELING PERSPECTIVES

It is not uncommon for counselors to receive calls from frustrated parents with a request to "straighten out" a youngster. It is understandable that parents would seek outside help in their discouragement with a difficult child. But counselors know that most often a mixed-up, rebellious child comes from a "mixed-up" marriage. Couples with weak or dysfunctional relationships have a difficult time rearing functional children, for children tend to reflect the same weaknesses inherent in individual parents and draw from the marriage partnership as a whole. It is from the parental example that children gain a lifelong compass, a degree of competence with organizational and financial skills, a measure of common sense, and a regard for self-denial and self-discipline.

SOURCE OF PATHOLOGY

Where do human beings learn to be emotionally and mentally healthy? Is it not from parents who possess these qualities? Where do children learn to be obnoxious, irritating, impatient, ornery, and selfish? The answer here too is the same: generally from their home life and their later peer group. What, then, makes the difference between healthy and dysfunctional children? Usually (not always) the disparity can be found in whether or not parents model for their children healthy individual male and female personalities and principles of sound male-female relationships.

SAME-SEX AND CROSS-GENDER INFLUENCE

Consider a young boy who grows up in a home with a father who is harsh, cruel, abusive, and somewhat distant. What impact do you think that father will have on his young son's sense of masculinity and maleness, on his sense of competence? Would a boy growing up in such an environment develop healthy, masculine traits that would prepare him well for the character traits required in his own marriage and future parenthood?

Could a young girl grow up in a home with a verbally and physically abusive mother and yet mature into a young woman without a warped sense of what constitutes femininity and the ability to relate well to men? Could such a young woman appreciate her divine attributes as a daughter of God and then anticipate motherhood herself when having children has not been satisfying to her own mother? Quite unlikely. How desperately children need parents who model unity and complementary strengths! We do not have to be perfect parents, obviously, but we do need to present a model of charity if we expect our children to mature in their own endowments of gender traits.

OPPOSITE-SEX GENDER INFLUENCE

Not only do parents influence children of their own gender, but they impact the opposite as well. It is from wonderful fathers that girls develop a sense of love and respect for men, and at the same time a confidence in their own feminine traits to complement those of men. It is from mothers who love their sons that young boys grow up to respect womanhood and motherhood and want to treat well those they date because of their own love and respect for their mother.

As a teacher of young people I frequently see those who want to avoid marriage and family because of their experiences in a dysfunctional home. More specifically, when students reveal that their parents' marriage has been shaky, they are more prone to postpone their own courtship. Such sons and daughters see few expressions of love and affection between Mom and Dad and they know something is missing. In some cases the parents are fairly hostile to each other, while a number are abusive verbally as well as physically. There will always be those who will say, "I have never seen my folks show any affection to each other."

Children are close observers of their parents. Often when young children see their parents argue, they are convinced that they are going to divorce and will often ask one parent, "Are you and Daddy going to divorce?" When young people hear adults extol a temple marriage—sometimes pleading for the children to marry there—and yet the parent model is dysfunctional, a temple marriage appears to them to be a mockery or outright hypocrisy. Such children often conclude that if a temple marriage has not brought their own parents happiness, perhaps a temple marriage isn't all it is advertised to be. The prospect of marriage and parenthood appears too threatening or intimidating for those with parents who have fallen into negative habits.

When children observe that the most important ordinance of the gospel—marriage—is not bringing happiness to their own parents, such children are more prone to turn away from the "faith that our fathers have cherished." The tragedy is that they may lose faith in the gospel because it lacks the power, as they see it, to bring their parents happiness. Then, those with a poor example of home life seek happiness outside the gospel framework. This quest cannot be ultimately successful, for true happiness, born of the Spirit of the Lord, cannot be found outside the plan of salvation.

For individuals from homes without a healthy marital example grounded in gospel principles the search becomes a fearful task, and this causes many to lose hope of finding happiness through marriage. Alternatively they may seek intimacy without commitment by imitating marriage—living with someone. Over the years the number of couples cohabiting has jumped alarmingly. Though these souls may seem to answer nature's mating call, they are making a mockery of what God intended for his children. By avoiding childbirth and the responsibilities associated with parenthood they cheat themselves of the true joy that comes to men and women through their offspring. Often we see children from such homes marry and divorce and marry and divorce, or they live in trial marriages because the idea of the marriage commitment frightens them. Unfortunately such practices can lead to a loss of their own salvation.

Here is how one student saw value in his parents' relationship:

> I always knew that my mother and dad loved each other; I never had to wonder about it. They worshiped each other, and it was obvious to us kids that their relationship was rock-solid. They always made it clear by both words and actions. Seeing the love that they had for each other and for each one of their children was so wonderful to see. My father took extra jobs to help support our family so that my mom could be at home. He never wanted her to have to work outside of the home, for our family was too important to him to trust to outsiders. Although my mom didn't have a "career," she was busier than most people I knew who had careers. She was constantly involved in church callings, volunteer work in the hospitals, baby-sitting, sewing, cooking, cleaning, driving, shopping, but most of all loving us.

Another student shared this observation:

> My father loves my mother dearly. When President Benson stated, "Flowers on special occasions are wonderful, but so is your willingness to help with the dishes, change diapers, get up with a crying child in the night, and leave the television or newspaper to help with dinner," he described my father perfectly. My mother is the queen of our home and he treats her that way. I love being at home with my parents and hope that I can love my husband as my father loves my mother.

John, another student, had these comments about his parents:

> My father really loves my mother. I can see it in the way he looks at her, the way he treats her, and the way he supports her. He has sacrificed so much so that she could be our mother. He takes her out on dates every Friday night, tells her all the time she is beautiful, and he always wants her to spend more money

on herself. I also know my father loves all us children with all his heart.

Earlier tonight on the phone, he told me of a story that occurred in the recent flooding in Southeast Texas, where I am from. A man's car was caught in the flood, and his family was stuck inside. He pulled his wife and one of his children out of the car safely. But when he pulled his eighteen-month old baby out of the car, he got hit by a wall of water and let go of the baby. I could tell my dad was deeply affected by this, as he told me, "They would have to rip my arm off before I would let go of my wife or one of my children!" I can feel his love in so many ways.

Robert, a senior at BYU, observed his father's treatment of his mother when she made a mistake:

On one occasion, my mother wanted to help out on the farm. She was driving the tractor for my dad and ended up knocking down a line of fence posts when she popped the clutch on the tractor. Later that same day she went to drive the hay boys home and ended up tearing the back door off our car. She started crying because she knew she had caused a lot of damage that resulted in a loss of money that we did not have. My dad never raised his voice or chewed her out in any way. He knew that she felt bad enough already and he understood that her intentions were good. He held her and loved her.

How do you suppose children from homes like these will function in their own marriage and parenting experiences? It is clear that the seeds of personality and sociability are sown in the home environment. Healthy attitudes concerning the purpose and meaning of life, God, family, sex roles, self, values, gospel principles, self-discipline, and righteousness stem from family values taught by parents who love each other and who pass on to their children these character values. Through parent-child conversations, teaching moments, questions and answers in a climate of calm and objective inquiry, and family home evenings, parents pass on worthwhile patterns of behavior and ideas that influence their own children and will be passed on to the next generation. Society is strengthened when individuals are "homegrown" by mature parents who give their children their best efforts. Here is the pattern: Healthy children come from healthy parents who replace themselves with children who are healthy in mental, emotional, and spiritual qualities of life.

8

Use of Agency Is Governing Factor

Perspective Eight: Ordinances do not supersede agency.

Many Christians believe that a confession of faith in Christ as their personal Savior is the only requirement for heaven's entrance. Though Latter-day Saints agree that grace *is* very important, we are fond of quoting the Apostle James that "faith without works is dead" (James 2:20). Though Nephi put the grace/works controversy in the proper context (see 2 Nephi 25:23), when it comes to temple marriage we seem to have the same kind of mind-set as our evangelical friends. We act as if a temple marriage is some type of "superglue" that unites couples together forever whether or not they like each other in this life.[23]

I have often felt that a definition of "hell" would go something like this: At the final judgment the Lord says: "Brother (or) Sister Jones, I'm sorry that marriage and family life were not good experiences for you. You certainly did not enjoy living as husband and wife, and your children did not bring you much happiness either. In fact, we were embarrassed to look in on you and your family. It was unfortunate that marriage was not something that you two enjoyed when it was designed to bring only happiness and joy to you. However, we have just held a council and decided to let you two live together forever anyway. Best wishes to you!"

I think most of us would admit that such a decision would be "hell," if the two people did not enjoy being together in mortality. And clearly that is not the way it will operate, either. We must be qualified for exaltation by ordinances, faithfulness, humility, and a genuine desire to be together as eternal companions, or we will find ourselves alone and separate for a long period of time![24]

Earlier I quoted Elder Joseph Fielding Smith on the seriousness of divorce. A point he made was that married couples who gain exaltation will "enter the celestial kingdom without the frailties and weaknesses of mortality." This conveys the idea that individuals will either make necessary changes in their character to conform to a celestial standard or they will not achieve that degree of glory. A man or woman who will not bring his or her behavior into conformity with celestial requirements will not attain the highest degree of glory. Wilford Woodruff reported this sermon by President Brigham Young:

> Some women say I do not want to live with my Husband in Eternity. They need not trouble themselves about it for she will not be troubled with him in Eternity unless he keeps the Commandments of God & if He goes to the Celestial Kingdom & she is not worthy of it, she will not be troubled with him for she will not go there. One man will say I do not want to go to heaven if such a man goes, but no one need be troubled about such matters for they will not go to Heaven themselves unless they are worthy & they will not meet any one there that is not worthy. (Wilford Woodruff's Journal, 1833–1898, spelling retained.)

On another occasion, President Young taught this principle:

> I think it has been taught by some that as we lay our bodies down, they will so rise again in the resurrection with all the impediments and imperfections that they had here; and that if a wife does not love her husband in this state she cannot love him in the next. This is not so. Those who attain to the blessing of the first or celestial resurrection will be pure and holy, and per-

fect in body. Every man and woman that reaches to this unspeakable attainment will be as beautiful as the angels that surround the throne of God. If you can, by faithfulness in this life, obtain the right to come up in the morning of the resurrection, you need entertain no fears that the wife will be dissatisfied with her husband, or the husband with the wife; for those of the first resurrection will be free from sin and from the consequences and power of sin. (*JD* 10:24.)

Ordinances do not supersede agency—that is my point here. Many times I hear individuals (usually women) say, "If I have to be married to (and she names her husband), I would rather be in the terrestrial (or telestial) kingdom. They sound as if a temple marriage will put them together without regard to anyone's wishes or common sense. But as Elder Robert D. Hales taught: "An eternal bond doesn't just happen as a result of sealing covenants we make in the temple. How we conduct ourselves in this life will determine what we will be in all the eternities to come." And then he made this important point: "To receive the blessings of the sealing that our Heavenly Father has given to us, we have to keep the commandments and conduct ourselves in such a way that our families will want to live with us in the eternities. The family relationships we have here on this earth are important, but they are much more important for their effect on our families for generations in mortality and throughout all eternity" (*Ensign,* November 1996, p. 65).

In an earlier writing, I related this true story:

Paul and Clara were an older couple who had been married for over thirty-five years. As I visited with them on several occasions, it became clear to me that their marriage was a disaster and had been for many years. Yet they had stayed together and reared a number of children. Though they were religiously active, their marriage, from nearly every aspect, was in shambles. As I met with them several times, they seemed intent on cataloging each other's sins in front of me. As soon as one took a breath, the other began his or her list of offenses.

I listened patiently until I felt that I had the courage to intervene, and interrupted their mutual bash session. "Excuse me," I said, "but in observing you two, I'd like to share an observation. You realize, of course, that in what I say I am not the final judge; the Lord will do that. But if the Judgment were held today, and the Lord called me to be a witness, let me tell you what I would say that I see. I would say that you both seem to have set a course for the telestial kingdom. I think the two of you have offended the Spirit of the Lord so badly by the way you treat each other that surely the heavens must weep at what they see. You have had the gospel your entire lives, yet you have missed its major theme. You have become so critical and devastating in your comments to each other that you ought to be ashamed to call yourselves Latter-day Saints. And if I am embarrassed at the way you censure each other, I can imagine how the Lord must feel.

"Paul," I said, looking him straight in the eye, "I don't think you understand the nature of the priesthood you hold. You have made a mockery of its beauty, influence, and power, especially as it relates to being Clara's husband.

"Clara," I said, turning to her, "after all these years of living with Paul, you seem to have no idea what makes a man tick, how to lift and inspire him to be a better companion to you."

Looking at both of them now, I continued: "The two of you have used your marital years to destroy rather than strengthen each other. Consequently, as I see it, you have only another twenty, maybe thirty years left to live with each other. Then one of you will die and that will be the end of your experience with marriage. Never again, through all eternity, will either of you live in a marriage relationship. I think"—I paused, hoping this next thought would sink in—"you will look back at these years with sadness for what might have been. I think you two will wish that you had made some different choices along the way. Of course, you have your agency; you may do as you please. And up until now you seem to have wanted to use it to devastate each other.

"On the other hand," I said, in an effort to bring something positive out of the whole mess, "wouldn't it be great on

Judgment Day to have the Lord say, 'You two had a rough thirty-five years, didn't you! And then you made some wonderful changes. You came to realize what mortal life, agency, and my atonement were all about, and the past thirty years have been a complete reversal from those earlier ones. Thank you for making the necessary changes! Thank you for doing what needed to be done in order to qualify for the highest degree of the celestial kingdom. Thank you for making my atonement worth the effort. I want to welcome you into a society of people who love their companions as you two now do, a society of couples who have conducted their lives so that they want and are eligible to be together forever.'"

I waited, holding my breath, thinking that they might run out the door offended. Instead, to my surprise, they both bowed their heads and began to weep. Paul took Clara's hand and apologized—right there in front of me. She reached out to him and accepted his embrace. Both admitted that the Lord must be disappointed with them; that they had treated each other terribly; that they had a long way to go but that they could do better—indeed, they *would* do better. Their apologies were accepted, and forgiveness was extended. They committed to each other that they would make the necessary changes. They seemed determined to turn things around. (From *Strengthening Your Marriage and Family,* pp. 1–3.)

Elder Marion G. Romney shared his perspective of a vision of the Prophet Joseph Smith:

Sometimes, however, because of our lack of understanding and appreciation of them [the fruits of the gospel], I am persuaded that we take too much for granted. We assume that because we are members of the Church we shall receive as a matter of course all the blessings of the gospel. I have heard people contend that they have a claim upon them because they have been through the temple, even though they are not careful to keep the covenants they there made. I do not think this will be the case.

We might take a lesson from an account given by the

Prophet of a vision of the resurrection in which he records that one of the saddest things he had ever witnessed was the sorrow of members of the Church who came forth to a resurrection below that which they had taken for granted they would receive. (Marion G. Romney, *Improvement Era*, November 1949, p. 754.)

In my university classes I have students write papers on their parents and family background. I ask them to evaluate the strengths and weaknesses of their father and mother as individuals and as a married couple, to describe their parents' marriage and what they want to duplicate in their own marriage from that of their parents, and what things they do not want to bring into their relationship.

Quite often students will share that their parents have only a shell of a marriage, and a number of them will admit that their parents do not even sleep together. I usually write a note on such students' papers asking them to stop by my office. When they do, I ask them for a few more details as to why they think their parents do not sleep together (maybe one sleeps in a separate bed because of snoring). I ask them why their parents, who don't like each other enough to sleep together, don't divorce, and the answer will usually be, "Because they were married in the temple!" Somehow these parents have the notion that though they may not like each other in this life, as long as they were married in the temple there will come a time beyond death when they will be madly in love with each other! (I presume that is when they think their spouse will find out that they were right all along. Or that the Lord will agree with their position and call the spouse to repentance or allow them to find someone worthy of them.) Oh how little we seem to know about love and charity as it exists for those of a celestial spirit.

Such people need to humble themselves, apologize, and take responsibility to repent of their sins and bring their union into a state where it has a chance to be eternal in nature. Of course, sleeping together is not the ultimate indicator of a strong marriage, for married companions share love in non-sexual ways too;

but physical and emotional intimacy are fairly good barometers of the quality and progress of a marriage. The Lord designed the sexual union not only as the way new life is created but also to be a way of expressing mutual feelings of love and appreciation ("Honey, I love being married to you, it is so wonderful to be your companion").

What a shame that people who have the privilege to be married in the temple (relatively not many have had the opportunity in the history of the world) can't humble themselves sufficiently to have the Spirit of the Lord with them. As President Spencer W. Kimball counseled:

> If each spouse submits to frequent self-analysis and measures his own imperfections by the yardstick of perfection and the Golden Rule, and if each spouse sets about to correct self in every deviation found by such analysis rather than to set about to correct the deviations in the other party, then transformation comes and happiness is the result. . . .
>
> For every friction, there is a cause; and whenever there is unhappiness, each should search self to find the cause or at least that portion of the cause which originated in that self. . . .
>
> Love is like a flower, and, like the body, it needs constant feeding. The mortal body would soon be emaciated and die if there were not frequent feedings. The tender flower would wither and die without food and water. And so love, also, cannot be expected to last forever unless it is continually fed with portions of love, the manifestation of esteem and admiration, the expressions of gratitude, and the consideration of unselfishness. ("Marriage and Divorce," BYU Devotional, September 7, 1976, pp. 6–7.)

REPENTANCE, THE KEY TO STRONGER MARRIAGES

When some of our recent prophets focused their prophetic insight on the reasons for marriage and divorce in the Church, President Spencer W. Kimball concluded that "every divorce is the result of selfishness" while President Ezra Taft Benson called pride the main culprit. President Gordon B. Hinckley has said:

I find selfishness to be the root cause of most [divorces]. I am satisfied that a happy marriage is not so much a matter of romance as it is an anxious concern for the comfort and well-being of one's companion. Selfishness so often is the basis of many problems, which are a very serious and real factor affecting the stability of family life. Selfishness is at the root of adultery, the breaking of solemn and sacred covenants to satisfy selfish lust. Selfishness is the antithesis of love. It is a cankering expression of greed. It destroys self-discipline. It obliterates loyalty. It tears up sacred covenants. It afflicts both men and women.

Too many who come to marriage have been coddled and spoiled and somehow led to feel that everything must be precisely right at all times, that life is a series of entertainments, that appetites are to be satisfied without regard to principle. How tragic the consequences of such hollow and unreasonable thinking! (*Ensign,* May 1991, p. 73.)

Counseling with couples with marital problems confirms the wisdom of these prophets. The major problem with these twin plagues, as I see them, is that individuals so afflicted do not take personal responsibility to repent and change their own behavior. Selfish and proud individuals are convinced that they are adequate, it is their spouse who is the major cause of their mutual unhappiness. They want the other person to admit their guilt, make changes to suit them, and then, they reason, maybe some progress can be made.

I am convinced that repentance is the most difficult principle of the gospel for us to live—especially in these days when we have been so blessed temporally. We are particularly prone to these twin spirit-killers, selfishness and pride, when our hearts are hardened by the ease of our lives. It seems to be the age-old theme that is so clear from the Book of Mormon that when prosperity brings a comfortable lifestyle, we forget God. (See Helaman 12:1–6—the best scripture to summarize this point.) It is not that the principle of repentance is difficult to understand or comprehend, but to actually carry it out, frequently in the form of an apology, is extremely difficult for most of us.

There are at least two reasons why it is hard for most of us to repent: (1) we do not want to take responsibility for our mistakes or poor behavior; and (2) we find it difficult to clear a misunderstanding without justifying or explaining why our behavior was the fault of someone or something else. To say: "I'm sorry. I made a terrible (dumb, unthinking) mistake, and I will do better. Please forgive me,"—this seems to be the challenge. I know because I struggle with it personally and I teach the principle constantly.

Let me illustrate. To repent of nasty words or comments spoken to one's spouse, true repentance would sound like this (assuming a genuine heart): "Honey, I said some pretty mean things this morning to you and I haven't felt good about it all day. I need to ask your forgiveness. I'm sorry I got angry. I can do better than that and I will not let it happen again." Or, "I said some pretty dumb things this morning. I'm sorry. I was careless and I just want you to know that what I said is not what I really feel; that it is not where my heart really is. I love you, and I'm sorry for my unthoughtfulness. I promise it won't happen again."

How would *you* say it? Perhaps you would use different words, but the intent is clear: You have erred and need to correct your offense with your spouse. In such circumstances we generally say something like this: "Honey, I said some pretty mean things to you this morning. But let me tell you *what you did* that made me so mad. When you attacked me with what you said. . . ." and suddenly we are on the defensive, trying to excuse our behavior rather than take responsibility for it! That is not repentance. It amounts to making us the victims of someone else's sin. "The reason I holler at my children is that they won't do anything unless I holler at them." "The reason I poked a hole in the wall is because you said . . ." as if what the other person did justified immature behavior on our part. "If only they would get some decent refs, then we would have won the ballgame . . ." The prisons are full of people who felt they had good reason to kill or maim someone else because of what that someone did.

Behavior is purposeful. And we seem to be able to come up with socially acceptable answers on why we did a particular thing or acted in a specific way; in fact, we are pretty good at creating them right on the spot! We are prone to excuse ourselves by rationalizing that "everyone else does it"; or we resort to placing our sins in the relativeness category: "You have to admit, I'm not as bad as . . ." We are prone to blame others for our weaknesses and inadequacies, or we accuse others of making us their victim if we were not promoted, lost a job, were sent home from a mission early, or flunked an exam.

I think that the ultimate test of integrity is when we receive a traffic ticket. Have you ever heard anyone say of their ticket: "I really deserved that. I was going too fast!" Have you ever heard a returned missionary say: "I was a terrible companion in the mission field? How they ever made it with me still amazes me!" Rather, we hear about the "crummy" or "dorky" companions a missionary had, but we never hear how the *other companion* felt about having *this person* as their companion. Do you recall ever hearing someone say: "It was really my fault that we were divorced. I was just a terrible husband (or wife) and I don't blame my spouse for wanting out of our marriage!" It would be rare indeed to have someone take the blame or responsibility, apologize, and get on with their life.

Now, let's think about you who are reading this. When was the last time you personally repented by taking responsibility and clearing something with another? By that I mean you either stopped a particularly nasty action or behavior or you started a new, more healthy pattern of doing something in a relationship. Can you remember genuinely expressing sorrow if you disciplined one of your children inappropriately, or raised your voice to your spouse, or were just downright irritable or cantankerous about something that, in the long run, was pretty trivial? I suspect you are a lot like me. It is difficult to admit to being wrong and then take responsibility to change, apologize, or correct the error.

The Nephites struggled with it. It took wars and the loss of a great deal of life before they could be humbled. Then when we compare their lifestyle with mine, I decide that, compared to the pride of the Nephites, we reek even more. They didn't have airplanes, watches, toilets, thermostats, polyester! And yet they were proud and arrogant to the point that they were finally destroyed by the Lord. (See Mormon 5:17–19.)

The term *road rage* is coming into our vocabulary. Here is a classic example of that kind of driving behavior from the Brigham Young University student paper, *Universe,* July 28, 1994, p. 6, "Policebeat":

> A driver, aggravated at what he thought was slow driving in front of him, drove in front of the driver and braked hard sparking a confrontation. The two cars battled on the road from Provo to Orem exchanging words and gestures. The drivers stopped to resolve the conflict with their fists, but when one driver saw he was physically overmatched he took a hammer from his car. The other driver responded by getting a pipe. Both drivers pounded the other's vehicle and wrestled on the ground. One driver broke away and told Orem police about the incident.

In my counseling with couples, my hope is that both will be anxious to improve the relationship, to find better ways of relating to each other, but they have a difficult time repenting. They have defended their behavior for so long prior to seeking help that their hearts are hardened. So instead of repenting, they will say, usually gritting their teeth as they say it: "Okay, I'll do the three things that you think are so important for me to do to improve this marriage, *if* [and they name the spouse] will do the three things you asked of him (or her)." Is that repentance? I'm afraid not. It sounds more like labor and management negotiating for a better contract.

Elder F. Burton Howard explained the problem:

> Unwillingness to accept the responsibility for and consequences of one's actions is an all too common condition in today's world. Who has not heard of the drunken driver who sues his host for allowing him to get drunk, or of the accident

victim who claims damages from the physician who tries to help
him? Perpetrators of the most heinous crimes often plead guilty
by reason of insanity or claim that they are victims of society's
ills. The homeless blame alcohol. Alcoholics blame genetic defi-
ciencies. Abusers and adulterers blame the broken homes of
their childhood. And there are enough who agree with them to
ensure that no one need feel terribly guilty for long if they
don't want to.

The habit of shifting the burden of guilt onto someone
else, while perhaps understandable in a secular setting, has more
serious consequences in a spiritual one. There, too, it has an ancient but not honorable tradition.

Cain blamed God when his sacrifice was not accepted. "I
was wroth," he said, "for his offering thou didst accept and not
mine" (Moses 5:38).

Laman and Lemuel blamed Nephi for nearly all their troubles
(see 1 Nephi 16:35–38). Pilate blamed the Jews when he con-
doned the crucifixion of the Savior, in whom he found "no fault"
(Luke 23:4; see also Matthew 27:24).

Even the very elite have sometimes succumbed to the
temptation to blame others for their disobedience or their failure to receive blessings. Aaron blamed the children of Israel
when Moses charged him with bringing a great sin upon them
by making a molten calf (see Exodus 32:19–24). And Martha
may have blamed Mary for depriving her of the Savior's presence on that indelible day in Bethany (see Luke 10:40).

Today the practice continues. We hear at every hand
phrases such as "My wife just doesn't understand me," "Loosen
up—everybody does it," or "It wasn't really my fault." The second great commandment (see Matthew 22:35–40) is breached
routinely by those who say, "He started it" or "She deserved
it." Teens and adults alike jokingly attempt to justify behavioral
lapses by saying, "The devil made me do it."

When faced with the consequences of transgression, rather
than looking to ourselves as the source of the discomfort which
always accompanies sin, many of us tend to blame someone
else. Rather than getting out of a vicious and senseless circle, we
fault our neighbor for our pain and try to pass it on. But to repent we must leave the circle.

The first step in the repentance process has always been simply to recognize that we have done wrong. If we are so hedged about by *pride, rationalization, machismo, or a misdirected sense of self-esteem* as to prevent us from ever admitting that we are part of the problem, we are in trouble. We then may not even know of our need to repent. We will have no idea whether the Lord is pleased with us or not and may become "past feeling" (1 Nephi 17:45). But all men, everywhere, must repent (see 3 Nephi 11:32). To fail to do so is to perish (see Luke 13:3; Helaman 7:28).

To excuse misconduct by blaming others is presumptuous at best and is fatally flawed with regard to spiritual things, for "we believe that men will be punished for their own sins, and not for Adam's transgression" (Articles of Faith 1:2). This means not only that we will not be punished for what Adam did in the Garden, but also that we cannot excuse our own behavior by pointing a finger to Adam or anyone else. The real danger in failing to accept responsibility for our own actions is that unless we do we may never even enter on the strait and narrow path. Misconduct that does not require repentance may be pleasant at first, but it will not be for long. And it will never lead us to eternal life.

[A] notion . . . widely shared is most often expressed by the phrase, "The end justifies the means." Such a belief, if left undisturbed and unchecked, can also impede the repentance process and cheat us out of exaltation.

Those who teach it are almost always attempting to excuse the use of improper or questionable means. Such people seem to be saying, "My purpose was to do good or to be happy; therefore, any little lie, or misrepresentation, or lapse of integrity, or violation of law along the way is justified." (F. Burton Howard, *Ensign,* May 1991, pp. 12–13.)

HOW REPENTANCE HEALS

When two people genuinely apologize to each other for their sins, mistakes, or personal lapses, this action has a healing effect of softening hearts and bringing a desire to rectify the problem, eliminate it, and see that it does not happen again.

When I sincerely apologize to my wife, she says something like: "Well, it wasn't your fault. I said some dumb things back to you that I'm not proud of either and I can certainly do better than that. I'm sorry." When both parties take responsibility for their actions, it is more likely that the situation will be resolved quickly and easily. When neither person is willing to apologize, take responsibility, admit error, insisting that they "were right all along," then defensiveness keeps the hurt feelings alive and they remain unresolved. They will fester and resurface again another day.

When it comes to serious sins such as adultery it is especially important for the offender to take responsibility and genuinely seek forgiveness. I recall asking a husband who had committed this grievous sin if he had ever, honestly, deep-down, genuinely apologized to his wife about his affair. He said, "Well, I think so," turning to her, "haven't I?" As I looked over at her, her head hung down and she was shaking her head—"no." Repentance for a sin of that magnitude would require genuine regret and an appreciation to the spouse for their willingness to forgive and go on. I think repentance would sound something like this:

"[Carol] I have made a serious mistake. I have broken my temple covenants and committed a horrible sin. I have broken your heart and the heart of our children and I am truly sorry. I'm sick about it and I need your forgiveness. I know it will be difficult for you, but if you think you could find it in your heart to forgive me, I want to make you a promise. You will never have to worry again about me making this mistake. You can count on me from now on. I was careless. I embarrassed you and me. I promise you that you will never again have to worry where I am or who I am with if I am late. I have learned my lesson and realize that I have offended you and our Heavenly Father. I desire to be forgiven by both you and the Lord. I'm so sorry. I am grateful that you are willing to stay with me and help me come back. I want you to know that I will do it. I will make this up to you, somehow. Please forgive my stupidity. I promise you that you now have a husband and father back where he belongs and I'll do my best to make it up to you."

Unfortunately, that is not the usual response of the sinner. In private, this particular person justified his behavior in this way: "Well, we were having problems in our marriage and she wouldn't listen to my side of the issue—so I decided, "to h—— with her." If she was going to be that way, then I knew other people who cared more for me than she did. Besides, our house is a mess, she put on way too much weight, and I had a hard time feeling close to her. This other woman seemed to be more attractive and one thing led to another and. . . ." Obviously this is not repentance. It made it appear as if the wife was the one at fault rather than him. It was his wife that needed to change, or he might even be justified in doing the same thing again. He would not have been so careless if she hadn't. . . .

I truly believe that when individuals take responsibility and admit their sins, even in the serious case of adultery, if the husband would humble himself and genuinely repent, the wife could gain some insights of things that she could have done differently, ways she could have been more affectionate or loving, or treated him differently. When two people find it in their heart to apologize to one another, hearts are usually softened and reconciliation then is much easier to achieve.

REPENTANCE AND CHILDREN

Repentance is also important for parents to initiate with their children. But again it is very difficult. We are the parents. We must be right! Yet, my experience is that the parent will most likely need to initiate the process, for generally children are not going to come forward to correct a problem on their own. Adults must be "big enough" (humble) to work out difficulties that arise with their children. After emotions have subsided, why don't we, one on one, take responsibility for our part of the problem and initiate a conversation something like this:

"Jim (Carol), I'm sorry that I have not been a very good father (mother) to you. I have been (so busy, preoccupied, selfish, ornery, goofy), and I have not been a very good listener (been helpful, considerate, sensitive) to your feelings, nor have I shown you much love and caring. I want you to know that I am sorry; I love you with all my heart; you have been on my mind constantly lately, and I want you to know how much I desire to have a good relationship with you; in fact, more than anything else in the world. You and I are father and son (daughter) and I am embarrassed that I have been so stubborn and unapproachable. I will do better. I want to, and I can. Be patient with me. My hope and prayer is that I have not (lost your confidence, destroyed your faith in me) to the point where we can't put our relationship back where I think we both want it to be; like it used to be, and where I hope you would like it to be. I love you and I ask you to forgive me and let me try again to be a better dad (mother)."

Did you notice—no blaming or accusing the other? This is very hard to do unless we are filled with genuine caring and charity! But in this case the parent is humbled to the depths of his or her soul and wants to improve the relationship and is willing to do something about his or her part to repair the strain. Generally the "law of reciprocity" comes into play and the child, sensing a genuine desire on the part of the parent to change or improve a relationship, will begin to move in the direction of the parent who initiates the repentance process. Exceptions, of course, come when one has "repented" superficially repeatedly in the past so that the repentance is not believable or acceptable; the one being apologized to has been repeatedly "burned" following supposed reformation on earlier occasions; or if the relationship has been fractured badly, it will take time and love to repair the rift; or if the child's heart is so hardened that he thinks the parent is trying to "con" him or her into changing simply for the sake of the parent.

Even where the parent is not the biggest contributor to the problem, issues still need to be dealt with, and if the parent takes what responsibility he or she can for the present state of the relationship it will help to grease the repentance wheels for both parties without either losing face or being embarrassed. Besides, how important is face when we are dealing with family members when we have invited them to spend eternity with us?

I called a good friend on the phone one day for a visit only to learn that their fifteen-year-old boy had left home. Our conversation went something like this:

"Do you know where Stewart is?"

"Yeah, he is staying with a friend."

"Do you ever talk to him?"

"Oh, yeah, we talk on the phone every once in a while."

"What have you said to him?"

"I told him that if he comes home he is going to have to agree to get back to church, to get back to early morning seminary."

Now, is that what this son needs? A demanding father who insists that church rituals are the first priority in restoring the son back home? No. Such demands are not going to accomplish their desire. What has to happen is for the father to repent, to take whatever responsibility he can for the fractured relationship, express love to his son, and seek an opportunity to get together and work out an acceptable solution. No doubt the son, after a month of living away from home, was embarrassed to be at a friend's where it would be awkward for both the son and the friend's parents harboring him. Surely those parents must question what their position should be in this case, and they would be relieved if the boy decided to bridge the gap with his parents and move out of their place and get back home. I would suggest that the solution must sound something like this:

"Stewart, it has been a month since you left. I have been sick to my stomach for a month and I don't think your mom has slept at all. I feel terrible that you felt you had to leave our home, that you felt so frustrated with me that you just needed to get away. I'm embarrassed about the whole thing. Your mom hasn't stopped crying since you left and I haven't had much sleep either. I realize that I made some major mistakes with you. I'm sorry. I know that I can do better than I have in the past; I want to do better and I will do better. I love you with all my heart and I'm sorry that you felt you needed to get away from home to find some peace. Please, can we get together and discuss what we can do to get this situation resolved?"

Obviously these feelings and comments have to be genuine; they can't be manufactured or forged. They can't be used to manipulate or con the other person. They must be real. There must be genuine feelings of wanting to do better on the father's part if the relationship is to improve. Even though the dad is only responsible for part of the problem (most likely), he must take responsibility for *some* of the problem. If it is the mother and daughter or father and daughter relationship, the same principle applies. Only repentance has the power to change relationships, to restore them to wholeness again, to bring people together or to reconcile. Only then does healing begin.

It takes the power of the Atonement (accessed through repentance) to accomplish this great miracle. Forgiveness must be freely given when repentance is proffered. No wonder the Lord instructed: "Wherefore, I say unto you, that ye ought to forgive one another; for he that forgiveth not his brother [or wife, or son, or daughter] his trespasses standeth condemned before the Lord; for there remaineth in him the greater sin." The Lord has said, "I, the Lord, will forgive whom I will forgive, but of you it is required to forgive all men." (D&C 64:9–10.)

Perhaps President Joseph F. Smith said it best:

Fathers, if you wish your children to be taught in the principles of the gospel, if you wish them to love the truth and understand it, if you wish them to be obedient to and united with you, love them! and prove to them that you do love them by your every word or act to them. For your own sake, for the love that should exist between you and your boys—however wayward they might be . . . when you speak or talk to them, do it not in anger, do it not harshly, in a condemning spirit. Speak to them kindly; get them down and weep with them if necessary and get them to shed tears with you if possible. Soften their hearts; get them to feel tenderly toward you. Use no lash and no violence, but argue, or rather reason—approach them with reason, with persuasion and love unfeigned. . . . get them to feel as you feel, have interest in the things in which you take interest, to love the gospel as you love it, to love one another as you love them; to love their parents as the parents love the children. You can't do it any other way. (*Gospel Doctrine,* Deseret Book, 1977, p. 316.)

Repentance has the power to renew relationships, and sometimes it is the only power that will.

9

Selfishness and Pride

Perspective Nine: Selfishness and pride are the twin plagues that destroy marriages and families.

I think most of us would admit that we are frequently guilty of being selfish and proud as long as no specifics were mentioned. When pressed to list examples or areas where we might act selfishly or proudly, being specific, I've learned, it is a bit more difficult. It happens this way:

When couples go to a counselor each person wants to be seen as the normal partner in the relationship, to make it seem as if the other spouse is the cause of the mischief or trouble. The dialogue may go something like this.

"Brother Brinley, I know I am not perfect, but—"

I interrupt. "You say you are not perfect?"

"Heavens, no."

"Can you give me an example of something you are not perfect in?"

"Well, there are a lot of things."

"I suppose so, but can you give me one example so that I might get a handle on what you would label imperfect."

"Certainly."

Long pause. Nothing. Awkward. Silence. Or the person will mention some trivial issue, something so minor as to be humorous if it were not so serious. (I don't wear a seatbelt; I'm later than usual coming home sometimes; I don't call when I'm going to be late.) People are reluctant to admit any major wrongdoing because they have justified in their own minds their past actions, or they don't want to give the spouse any more ammunition with which to injure them.

Over the years of listening to people catalog their partner's faults, I can't remember even one spouse stopping the other during the "litany" of faultfinding and saying:

"Honey, I'm sorry. Do you mean that for [however long the offense has been occurring] years I have been hurting you with my sarcasm? I am sorry. I was ashamed to listen to you recite to Dr. Brinley the things I did to hurt you. I promise you that from now on that will never again happen in our marriage."

Unilateral admissions or confessions are as rare these days as the spotted owl! It is difficult for us to admit that we have offended someone else because, to us, our behavior seemed so natural. So we think the other person is too sensitive.

Some time ago I began making lists of things that I think indicate just how selfish we really are. After all, if President Spencer W. Kimball felt that "every divorce is the result of selfishness on the part of one or the other or both parties to a marriage" (*The Teachings of Spencer W. Kimball,* p. 313), then we need to pay attention to what type of selfishness is going on in our marriage. If President Gordon B. Hinckley would say "I find selfishness to be the root cause of most of [divorce]" (*Ensign,* May 1991, p. 73), then we all need to examine ourselves on this matter of self-centeredness.

I would like to share the following lists with you. Rather than comment on each one, I will just list them and let you see if you can see the selfish or proud attitude behind each one. There may be some here that could be justified in certain cases, but. . . .

SINS OF SELFISHNESS AND PRIDE

1. A person who accepts an assignment or calling to home teach or visit teach, but does not do it, or does it the last day of the month.

2. A faculty member who wants to teach only what he wants to teach and at his time/room/schedule. "Don't give me an eight o'clock class."

3. A husband who complains when meals are not ready—as if his wife had nothing to do all day but prepare meals for his schedule.

4. Students who walk across lawns rather than use the sidewalks.

5. Students who drop the daily campus newspaper and inserts on the floor or in the classroom, apparently expecting someone else to pick it up and discard it.

6. Sports/TV fanatic—watches five hours/day—the average for the U.S.

7. Pornography viewing/overweight not due to genetics. Many a husband complains about his wife's weight when his own stomach is grossly distended over his belt!

8. A young man or older couple who will not serve a mission when the situation allows.

9. A person who brings a book to sacrament meeting in case the speaker is "boring"; a person who brings papers to correct or a book to read during a presentation by an outside speaker.

10. Couples who do not want more children when age and physical and mental health are such that they could have more children.

11. One who, after trying on clothes in a fitting room, leaves the clothing on the floor or chair rather than returning it to the racks.

12. Spouse who controls the remote control.

13. Participant in petty theft.

14. One who won't allow spouse any spending money.

15. One who gossips—but doesn't see it as gossip; rather it is "sharing information."

16. One who monopolizes conversations.

17. One arrogant about sports knowledge; opinionated beyond good sense in defending the trivial.

18. One who will not stop for the national anthem when it is played.

19. One with rude driving habits.

20. Driver who tailgates/flashes lights to change lanes when speed is already excessive.

21. One who talks to others during a movie/speaker's presentation.

22. A personality who "sucks the joy out of life daily," meaning that his temperament or obnoxiousness makes it difficult for those he lives with.

23. One who holds grudges—won't speak to family, relatives, or business associates, yet takes the sacrament weekly.

24. One who is tactless, blunt, critical—yet personal appearance, breath, or sensitivity of the critic is offensive to others.

25. Defensive person.

26. One who will not attend nearby temple.

27. One not into family history or research, but who loves TV.

28. One humble only when a crisis occurs (divorce papers filed, injury, cancer, children rebel).

29. One who will not accept suggestions or correction.

30. One who does not accept/fulfill Church callings.

31. One who will not visit inactive members/elderly.

32. Male who does not date/seek marriage partner at appropriate age/time—21–25.

33. Singles who are more interested in money/things/possessions than marriage, spouse, and children.

34. One who dominates, smothers, controls conversation or behavior of others.

35. One who will not initiate or participate in family home evening, or family prayers.

36. One with poor manners—sloppy, hurried eater.

37. One who won't pick up after self or make bed, thinks housework demeans.

38. One who is a leader but will not attend Saturday evening leadership session of stake conference.

39. One who withholds tithing/offerings.

40. Man who is too cheap to take spouse/family out for dinner/movie/activity occasionally.

41. One always late to meetings.

42. One who whistles or/and hollers when film breaks during movie.

43. One not interested in ideas/solutions of children or spouse.

44. One who displays anger and temper to control/punish others.

45. One who criticizes Church leaders who are freely giving their best efforts.

46. One mean-spirited, moody, ornery, loud, and swears.

47. One who does not attend campus devotionals even when General Authorities speak.

48. One worldly or extreme in music, dress, hairstyles.

49. Student who struggles with dress/grooming standards.

50. One who is contentious and argumentative but considers self spiritual.

51. One who dominates Sunday School or Church classes with comments.

52. One who buys expensive (more than quality) items to show off—cars/homes/gadgets.

53. One who leaves paper and trash behind.

54. One competitive in sports/games beyond good sense.

55. Rebellious one—won't wear seat belt/bike helmet.

56. One who takes offense easily.

57. One who will not apologize/repent/change behavior to please spouse/family.

58. Poor listener, especially with family members; always right.

59. One who gets emotional quickly, is temperamental.

60. One who constantly complains about his salary and benefits.

61. One with contentious, argumentative, combative nature.

62. One who exercises unrighteous dominion, bossy, controlling nature.

63. One whose self-esteem and happiness is tied to things or objects.

64. One who criticizes coaches/players/other drivers.

65. One with public image inconsistent with private acts.

66. One who does not recognize a loss of the Spirit.

67. One who interrupts others to correct trivial mistakes.

68. One inflexible, strongly opinionated—e.g.,—politics.

69. One moody, irritable, hostile.

70. Women who will not accept dates—angry at men, have given up on marriage.

71. One who will not subscribe to *Ensign/Church News,* but takes many secular magazines.

72. One who watches R-rated movies contrary to counsel.

73. One who goes into debt to buy things to impress others.

74. One who tells supervisor instead of person directly.

75. One stingy with compliments.

76. One who throws trash out car window.

77. One impatient with little children/teenagers.

78. One unfeeling, uncaring, unloving.

79. One who commits publicly but does not follow through.

80. One who considers self intellectual, searches mysteries with shallow doctrinal background.

81. One who flirts.

82. One who tears pages out of telephone book instead of making notes.

83. One whose loud music from car or apartment disturbs environment.

84. One who leaves trash under seat or in aisle after sporting event.

Some of these items listed may be a matter of simple unconsciousness or innocence rather than true selfishness, but most of us can, I hope, see ourselves in such actions. Thinking that many of us would not relate to these illustrations of selfish behavior, I made a list of selfish acts I have observed in marriage relationships that I have seen in trying to help steady the marital ship of others. I separated these by husband and wife examples:

Husband:

1. Critical of wife's appearance/weight/aging when he is substantially overweight.

2. Critical of wife's driving/not buying gas at the place he wants, insists on (saves a whole 30 cents to buy 10 gallons at 3 cents less) but burns $1 of gas to get there.

3. Critical of wife leaving the home lights on all night, of being on the telephone too long, or too many long distance calls to family members; and thermostat up past 68 degrees.

4. Leaves bathroom messy; won't put dishes into dishwasher; doesn't pick up dirty clothes; thinks of wife as a maid.

5. So fussy about everything being put away in its own little place, compulsive beyond good sense about placement.

6. Chintzy in expressing appreciation, gratitude, kindness to wife—yet wants sex on demand; critical of wife's sexual interest and technique.

7. If his kids spill anything on car seat/floor accidentally he is on a tirade—yet wouldn't say anything to a neighbor if he/she spilled.

8. Hoards money; won't let wife have much/be involved in management; criticizes her expenditures; yet will buy a new shotgun, golf set, car, toys.

9. Exchanges sex for money, trips, clothes/things.

10. Criticizes children—but to wife rather than to children. Expects wife to make corrections in "her" children.

11. Does not preside, conduct, or participate in family home evening, prayer, or family councils.

12. Temperamental—everyone in the family is nervous when he is around. When he is home, kids scatter or leave the house; when he is gone, it is a relief to all who live there.

13. Teaching techniques are based on temper, bullying tactics, rather than teaching in a gentle, kind way in a family gathering.

14. Irritable when he doesn't get his own way; expects wife to move schedule to always meet his.

15. Critical of wife's friends but not much of a companion to her, either. Doesn't take or make time for sharing ideas, feelings, thoughts, ways to improve family, children, or resolve difficult situations.

16. Critical of Church leaders, teachers, administration, yet won't take a calling or participate in Church activities.

17. Wife must handle all spiritual activities. Does not ask wife or children to pray with him. "If you want to pray, go ahead."

18. Critical of wife's weight/bust/legs after she has had children; pregnancies are difficult.

19. Publicly criticizes wife: interrupts/chastises/corrects/ridicules/belittles.

20. Treats other women better than his own spouse.

21. Nice to everyone outside family but a terror at home. The ward thinks he is one of the "nice guys." Children and wife know better.

22. Does not express non-sexual affection/kindness/appreciation to wife for her contribution to his life or their home.

23. Uses temper to control/scare/intimidate.

24. Workaholic—trying to earn more money, but actually avoids family responsibilities; "I don't know how to be a father but I do know how to work hard" becomes an excuse to avoid husband/father duties.

25. Swears/coarse language; impatient with mechanical things, children, teens; throws wrench across garage floor or wall.

26. Not involved in family discipline; avoids confrontations with children/teenagers.

27. Needs deodorant soap, aftershave, mouthwash.

28. Does not take counsel from spouse/children.

29. Reads/views pornography and wants wife to act like prostitute/wear prostitute clothing. Views pornography as okay as long as wife is his only partner.

30. Won't relinquish remote control.

31. When he has time off from work he does his thing—not family things or things with wife.

32. Husband wants wife to work to take the financial pressure off him, but he doesn't help out around the house any more than when she was home.

33. Makes decisions and informs wife of the decision. Not an equal partnership—especially on financial matters.

34. He sits in front of the TV till bedtime. No social life. She wakes him in time to go to bed.

35. After entertaining guests, he goes to bed and leaves her

with the dishes and cleanup. Says, "I've got a rough day tomorrow; I'd better get to bed; see you in the morning."

36. He is out in the car honking the horn while she is getting the little ones ready for church. He can't understand why she and the kids aren't ready to go, but doesn't help them—just honks.

37. He brags about spending time with the kids, but when he is with them he is critical of them and they don't like being with him.

38. When wife goes to church/social/club meetings, he's grumpy because he has to take care of the kids. "I have things to do too."

39. He doesn't allow his wife time with friends/activities that she likes/needs for therapy.

40. He doesn't carry any life insurance on himself; he could die and leave wife without any financial security.

41. He leaves newspaper all over the floor/table expecting her to pick up.

42. Treats wife like one of the kids; won't allow her to talk to certain people, say certain things, talk about finances.

Wife:

1. Unappreciative of husband's hard work to earn a living and bring money home. It is not easy to make a living; some jobs have little in the way of promotional opportunities.

2. Homecoming of husband is not a special event; no approaching for a hug/kiss/see how the day went, "I missed you."

3. Grumpy about housekeeping/homemaking responsibilities.

4. Uses sex as a weapon to hurt, reject, punish, reward.

5. Past menopause—no need for sex.

6. No backrubs/foot rubs, special treatment, deserts, meals.

7. Critical of husband's efforts when he tries to teach children/ responsibility.

8. Leaves disciplining up to husband; avoids confrontations with children. "Wait till your dad gets home."

9. Spends more time with children than with husband.

10. More interested in the house, furniture, cleanliness, than husband/children.

11. Critical of other women in the ward/neighborhood, catty/gossip.

12. Extravagant needs for clothes, furniture, vacations.

13. Housekeeping skills are not good and she has no desire to improve.

14. A poor teacher/student; not anxious to learn better ways to do things; uses anger/temper to get attention or to try to change others.

15. Careless in weight/body tone/hairstyle/exercise/eating habits. Married in the temple—attitude is "what does it matter—where can he go? What can he do without being excommunicated?"

16. Uncooperative in helping with family home evening/family council; critical of leadership.

17. Compares husband with her father/Church leaders; expresses disappointment.

18. Does not honor priesthood of husband—meaning she is critical of his efforts to bless children, manage money, and so on.

19. Not open to intimate encounters at other times of day/places. Affection/sex silly "at our age." "When is he going to grow up and stop thinking about sex all the time?"

20. Demands expensive/oversize home and furnishings.

21. Wife doesn't want to be tied to kids all day; works because being home is boring compared to social situations at work.

22. Complains if he does anything with his friends outside of home. Wants all of his time.

23. Not nice to his parents. Rude/doesn't speak/to his parents/family.

24. Won't leave kids/grandkids to go on mission/temple/get away on dates.

25. Needs to use deodorant, mouthwash, soap, perfume.

THINGS THAT PEOPLE WITH SOFTENED HEARTS DO

Now lest you think I only observe the negative traits of people, here is a list of things that people with a softened heart do:

1. Sensitive to new converts, inactives—invite to home, to dinner, to family home evening.
2. Sensitive to singles and single parents in the ward and neighborhood; invite to dinner, babysit so they can date, go out.
3. Write note to sacrament meeting speakers that particularly touch you; youth speakers—comment on specific ideas/talents/ thoughts.
4. Take blessing of baby down in shorthand; deliver to parents that evening.
5. Shovel sidewalks; pick up litter in street, ward/neighborhood.
6. Introduce self to visitors; strangers, individuals you don't know but would like to know.
7. Make comments in classes that are more tentative: "I'm not sure if I can say this right, but I think . . ." "I hope this doesn't sound insensitive, but I feel that . . ." "This may not be exactly right, but I have always thought that . . ." Leave room for new ideas/insights.
8. Letter to bishopric/stake presidency—appreciation for service to you/family.
9. Attend baptisms in ward; firesides. Someone has gone to a lot of trouble and is worried if anyone will show up. If too many distractions from family activities, tell someone kindly/gently.
10. Pick up litter/clothes that have fallen off racks.
11. Never criticize or put down spouse/children/family in public. Teach in family home evening; one on one; in private counsel. There are better ways to teach.
12. Smile at those you pass; a simple "Hi."
13. Touch those you love and appreciate—handshake, arm around, arm in arm, pat on the back, and so forth.

14. Direct expressions of love and appreciation.

15. Letters/phone calls to family, siblings, divorcees, single parents.

16. Turn off the TV and get involved with family.

17. Other than general conference, avoid Sunday TV unless a family thing.

18. Visit those in hospital/homebound/aged/and so on.

19. Write missionaries from ward. Bear testimony, send Book of Mormon with your family picture, message.

20. Don't be embarrassed to ask names when you forget; be honest in communications.

21. One on one with children—expressions of love.

22. Home/visit teach early in month—call to say hello as follow-up.

23. Be aware of non-member associates—not obnoxious, but genuine expressions of love and desire to share.

24. Speak highly of spouse and children to others—but not a constant subject!

25. Stay awake in meetings. (By sleeping we do a disservice to those who speak and those who may be visiting.)

26. Congratulate sustainees; thanks to released.

27. Scoutmaster/cubmaster—know who they are, express thanks.

28. Gospel doctrine/Relief Society/priesthood and Primary teachers—let them know when you or a child gained a new insight/idea.

29. Expressions of appreciation to co-workers.

30. Listen to what others say; write it down; get spelling of names right; use phone/mail/e-mail more to bless and thank.

31. Become a father/mother to children of single parents in ward (they need a role model/hero).

32. Sometimes only money can help (anonymous gift).

33. Ask bishop who in ward needs a visit, is lonely—and then go visit.

34. Get temple recommend early, at appointed times.

35. Pray appropriately: beginning of meeting/end of meeting.

36. Help children with reverence—times when they need to go out; times when they need to stay.

37. Don't walk in during musical number—at least to the front rows. Don't disturb Spirit.

38. Be on time for meetings.

39. Christlike traits: humility, meekness, love unfeigned, flexible, kind.

40. Character, the true aim of education—check self.

41. Puts away chairs/tables after activity.

All of us suffer from selfishness and pride. The prophets have told us so, and we live in a time when it is easy to be selfish and yet be able to justify it or rationalize it. Some of us take offense when one was not intended. I like the Prophet Joseph Smith's approach to not taking offense.

> I went one day to the Prophet with a sister. She had a charge to make against one of the brethren for scandal. When her complaint had been heard the Prophet asked her if she was quite sure that what the brother had said of her was utterly untrue.
>
> She was quite sure that it was.
>
> He then told her to think no more about it, for it could not harm her. If untrue it could not live, but the truth will survive. Still she felt that she should have some redress.
>
> Then he offered her his method of dealing with such cases for himself. When an enemy had told a scandalous story about him, which had often been done, before he rendered judgment he paused and let his mind run back to the time and place and setting of the story to see if he had not by some unguarded word or act laid the block on which the story was built. If he found that he had done so, he said that in his heart he then forgave his enemy, and felt thankful that he had received warning of a weakness that he had not known he possessed.
>
> Then he said to the sister that he would have her to do the same: search her memory thoroughly and see if she had not her-

self unconsciously laid the foundation for the scandal that annoyed her.

The sister thought deeply for a few moments and then confessed that she believed that she had.

Then the Prophet told her that in her heart she could forgive that brother who had risked his own good name and her friendship to give her this clearer view of herself.

The sister thanked her advisor and went away in peace. (Comments by Jesse W. Crosby in *They Knew the Prophet*, edited by Hyrum L. and Helen Mae Andrus, Bookcraft, 1974, p. 144.)

FIGHTING SELFISHNESS AND PRIDE IN OUR HOMES

Parents who love each other are able to fight these twin plagues more effectively, for where love exists it is best nurtured in an environment free from pride and self-centeredness. Loving couples learn to sacrifice for and respect each other, and their example increases the likelihood that such traits will pass to their children. Thus happily married people are more likely to have children who avoid selfishness and pride in their own marriages.

10

The Church and Family Life

Perspective Ten: The Church exists to help us succeed in our family life.

During a presentation to a group of Church singles on one occasion, an individual was quite agitated about "why the Church doesn't do more to help singles and marrieds succeed. Given our emphasis on marriage and family," the individual asked in front of the group, "why doesn't the Church provide marriage enrichment classes and post-marriage classes, require visits with the bishop before obtaining a divorce, give post-divorce counseling, help singles integrate more effectively into wards that are predominately family-oriented, etc., etc."

Her comments stuck with me for some time after that. We often hear people complain "why the Church doesn't . . ." I think I am beginning to understand why the Church does not want to create more "programs" even though they may sound laudable on the surface. For over thirty years I have taught a class entitled "The Teachings of the Living Prophets" at both an Institute level and at Brigham Young University. Instructing that course has required me to read the general conference talks and BYU speeches, Church magazines, and *Church News* remarks of the Brethren over the years. I can't think of any principle that they have not taught that would resolve our problems as individuals and as families. I think the Brethren do encourage bishops and other Church leaders to clear their schedules to give more individual help where it is clearly needed, to lead out more in helping individuals solve their problems; in fact, they have given much counsel to leaders on the need to follow through in areas where the Spirit inspires them to place emphasis. But it seems to me that we are missing some bedrock principles when we are anxious to have "the Church" be responsible for areas clearly within our own jurisdiction. Let me review areas where I think we could succeed in reducing programs rather than increasing them.

Principle #1: The Holy Ghost As a Personal Revelator. True growth comes from exercising our agency and experiencing the consequences of those choices whether good or not. We, of course, want to make wise decisions in order to experience the most joy and happiness possible. But we make mistakes, and that was why the Atonement was instituted from "before the foundation of the world." At baptism, we covenant with God to do our best to live gospel principles and he in turn allows us to have a member of the Godhead to help us live well our mortal stewardships. Counsel by this counselor is available to each one of us as a member of the Church. This personal Liahona is given to us to help us apply the principles of the gospel to our individual and collective family situations, becoming a personal revelator to that extent.

It was never the Lord's intention that the Church should take over our lives and dictate what we should or should not do. (That was the other plan!) Church leaders can help, counsel, advise, and give suggestions, but it is up to each of us to make decisions. It is through that system that we learn to grow and govern our own lives. It is for those decisions that we will someday be judged.

The Brethren are under a great responsibility to ensure that we understand basic gospel principles through the Church curriculum. "Verily I say unto you," the Lord said to the earliest First Presidency and Quorum of Twelve, "behold how great is your calling. Cleanse your hearts and your garments, lest the blood of this generation be required at your hands." (D&C 112:33.) I testify, after years of studying conference talks, that the Brethren are doing their job well.

But the thrust of individual gospel study is to help us solve our own problems. We each have the right to revelation and inspiration for our own individual lives and stewardships. Too many of us do not seek that inspiration, or receiving it, we ignore or discount it. We would rather have someone tell us what to do, who to marry, or to stay or not stay in a dysfunctional marriage or divorce. "In the plan of salvation God does for human beings only what they cannot do for themselves," wrote my former dean of Religious Education, Robert J. Matthews. "Man must do all he can for himself. The doctrine is that we are saved by grace, 'after all we can do'" (2 Nephi 25:23). (*A Bible! A Bible!*, Salt Lake City: Bookcraft, 1990, p. 186.)

"Spiritual independence and self-reliance is a sustaining power in the Church," said Elder Boyd K. Packer to those who would have the Lord (or the bishop) solve all their problems. "If we rob the members of that how can they get revelation for themselves? How will they know there is a prophet of God? How can they get answers to prayers? How can they know for *sure* for themselves?" (*Ensign*, May 1978, p. 92.)

Though prophets counsel, it is up to each of us to implement that which would be of most worth given our set of living conditions.

Principle #2: The prophets tell us that selfishness and pride— hard-heartedness—are the major problems that cause us suffering. One key given us by the Lord in order to avoid these twin marriage killers is to have every young man serve a mission, counsel given by President Spencer W. Kimball in 1974. Missions combat selfishness and pride in so many ways. As one student of mine observed:

> A few years ago, and even last year when I was a freshman (at BYU) dating young men prior to their missions, I regarded this advice of a mission as silly and not important for me to listen to. Now, however, I have a bit more perspective on this matter and realize how true this counsel is. When I compare guys who have returned from their missions with ones who haven't yet gone, I realize that a great deal of maturity and

growth comes from serving a mission. Besides, I think it is important for missionaries to be able to focus on their missions, and not be distracted by girlfriends and such. Now that I am older, I realize the importance of this counsel.

Missions are the best preparation for success in marriage and family life. Perhaps the most important thing we could do to strengthen our family relations is to implement the very wise counsel (if not commandment) that every young man who is worthy, normal, and capable, should serve a mission.

We are under covenant to establish a latter-day Zion. Where else can a young man in today's world (no military draft at the present moment) learn discipline, self-control, maturity, spirituality, and hard work that will serve him well in life as well as in marriage and family matters? No wonder the Lord has asked every young man in the Church to serve a mission.

Principle #3: Mothers make the difference. Another solution to present day problems is to allow mothers to be mothers! They are needed more to influence our children now than ever before. Perhaps not since the days of the stripling warriors in the Book of Mormon have we needed mothers who would take the responsibility of mothering seriously. This calling is the most important and yet difficult job on the planet. It requires every divine talent and ability that women possess to become effective mothers. Because of the stress on material needs, many women are going out into the work force to earn more money for their families while the children are off to expensive day care. The message from the Lord's prophets is that mothers with children at home should only work outside the home if that is essential to help provide for the family's *needs*, and that the contribution a mother makes to her family in today's society is worth far more than the monetary funds she could bring in to raise the standard of living. Think what mothers could do if their concentration was on their children: more young men (and women) would graduate from seminary and institute; more young men and women would serve missions, more young people would marry in the temple, more children would learn to stifle selfish impulses and unselfishly serve others, and more mature young men would be prepared to carry out our mission to share the gospel with the world.

President Ezra Taft Benson expressed these sentiments: "I say to all of you, the Lord has charged men with the responsibility to provide for their families in such a way that the wife is allowed to fulfill her role as mother in the home" (*Ensign*, November 1987, p. 49). President Spencer W. Kimball pleaded: "The Lord knows . . . that through circumstances beyond their control, some mothers are faced with the added responsibility of earning a living. These women have God's blessing, for he knows of their anguish and their struggle." (*Ensign*, November 1978, p. 103.)

President Gordon B. Hinckley has reminded us:

> There are some women (it has become very many in fact) who have to work to provide for the needs of their families. To you I say, do the very best you can. I hope that if you are employed full-time you are doing it to ensure that basic needs are met and not simply to indulge a taste for an elaborate home, fancy cars, and other luxuries. The greatest job that any mother will ever do will be in nurturing, teaching, lifting, encouraging, and rearing her children in righteousness and truth. None other can adequately take her place.
>
> It is well-nigh impossible to be a full-time homemaker and a full-time employee. (*Ensign*, November 1996, p. 69.)

Principle #4: Avoid pornography—the great plague of our day. I suppose nothing is more heart-rending and destructive to a marriage than to listen to a young bride tell of movies and videos her husband brings home to view. President Gordon B. Hinckley has been an advocate to stay away from pornography. Listen to his warning:

> This stuff is titillating, it is attractive, it is made so. Leave it alone! Get away from it! Avoid it! It is sleazy filth! It is rot that will do no good! You cannot afford to watch video tapes of this

kind of stuff. You cannot afford to read magazines that are designed to destroy you. You can't do it, nor even watch it on television. . . . Stay away from it! Avoid it like the plague because it is just as deadly, more so. The plague will destroy the body. Pornography will destroy the body and the soul. Stay away from it! It is as a great disease that is sweeping over the country and over the entire world. Avoid it! I repeat, avoid it! Avoid it! (Priesthood session, Jordan Utah South Regional Conference, March 1, 1997, in *Church News,* October 4, 1997, p. 2.)

Often the consequence of viewing this trash is a husband who wants his wife to try every sexual technique at a frequency he demands after fanning the flames of his sexual desires. Or I find husbands sending away to catalogue stores to order provocative and demeaning clothing, and then insisting their wives wear the items; or a husband expects his sweetheart to perform disgusting sexual acts. It is a sad commentary to listen to women whose husbands become sex addicts. They quickly lose respect for their husbands, who not only dishonor their priesthood but are surely losing the Spirit of the Lord in their lives and perhaps endangering their salvation.

A new bride told me how her first husband would stay up late at night to watch "all of the sexy movies on Showtime late at night. It disgusted me to see that he was watching them so I went to bed. It made him mad that I would not play the sex kitten he was looking at on the screen. We divorced soon thereafter."

Of course sexual intimacy is an important part of every married couple's love and physical expression of affection and caring. But this relationship is to be kept within the bounds the Lord has set, within guidelines that do not offend the Spirit of the Lord. When you consider the potential our wives have to rise to great spiritual heights in the eternities, the desire should be to treat a wife with great respect and dignity and not to offend her by demanding sexual acts contrary to good sense and spiritual sanction.

Principle #5: Your source of happiness as a married couple will come from watching your children grow to maturity, strong in their testimony of the gospel of Jesus Christ, and who pattern their own marriage and spiritual practices after you two. Years ago I listened as a General Authority told a group of Institute and Seminary teachers that in teaching the youth of the Church we ought to encourage them to look for a marriage partner who had a great desire to become a parent. At the time I did not understand the wisdom behind that comment. Now I do. I have learned that a wife who is a good mother sows the seeds of her husband's love and devotion to her. Of course, being a wife to her husband is her first priority, but so much of our lives are wrapped up in the lives of our children. When a husband finds that his spouse is an effective parent, he is not only relieved as a husband but is also humbled as he watches the profound talents of his wife unfold.

An important aspect of strengthening relationships with children comes from teaching them what they must know in order to function in their own spirituality. That involves working with them on scripture study, prayer, expressing affection, service, caring for other family members, instilling in them a work ethic, money management skills, feelings and emotions, conversation with others—especially other adults—a sensitivity to other people, and so on. When parents take time to teach their children right from wrong, children love their parents for taking the time to love them and to teach them. That is the focus behind the Lord's reinstitution of family home evening in 1965. It is during this special time together that family members learn from each other through lessons, playing together, building an environment for safely risking feelings and ideas, and coming to know the very heart and soul of each individual family member. What a wonderful way to build strong family relations and values into the hearts of our children! That will come, of course, if family home evening is consistently held at home and it is an enjoyable time for everyone.

Someone has said, "Family home evening is the only argument that begins and ends with prayer." That sacred time, once a week, is the time the Lord has given us to develop a closeness to each other and strengthen family ties. How can we expect to be together forever if we don't take the time to love each other here in this life? The First Presidency has promised the Saints that if they will conscientiously follow this weekly program with the intent of building warm and close family relationships "ninety-nine out of a hundred," would not go astray (see introduction to family home evening manuals, #1, #3, #5).

Principle #6: Be positive in your home with spouse and children. Put your arm around your children and love them and help them to understand the need for discipline, for family and societal rules. I am a believer that "all behavioral problems are relationship problems." Relationships are strengthened by expressions of love like these:

"It was so much fun to be with you."

"Thanks for going with me."

"How could I be so lucky as to have you for a son/daughter?"

"That's terrific—how did you know how to do that?"

"What a sweetheart you are."

"I love you with all my heart."

"What do you think we should do to help Mom?"

"Now I know why the Lord sent you to me."

"I never had so much fun."

"You are growing up so strongly in the gospel."

"You remind me of your mom/dad—what a jewel."

"Thanks for being my son."

"I wish I'd have been at your level of spirituality when I was your age."

"Let's do it again sometime."

"You really have some great skills in tennis/bowling/ping pong. Where did you learn to play like that?"

Lots of physical touching between individuals, and eye contact and listening ears, is needed in every family. Randal Wright shared this story in an earlier publication:

All of us as human beings have a basic need to feel loved. Not only does parental touch in the form of holding and hugging signify love to a child, but mounting evidence from research confirms that physical affection is an important physiological need. When children feel love within the context of their family setting, they feel secure and confident in their own abilities, and therefore their behavior is more consistent with parental values and ideals. When this need for love and affection goes unmet, however, there is the probability that children will seek attention, love, and affection elsewhere. For teenagers this quest becomes especially dangerous because they often turn to members of the opposite sex (and sometimes the same sex) to meet these needs. The adversary uses this basic human requirement to entrap susceptible youth in immorality.

President Ezra Taft Benson referred to this when he said, "I recognize that most people fall into sexual sin in a misguided attempt to fulfill basic human needs. We all have a need to feel loved and worthwhile. We all seek to have joy and happiness in our lives. Knowing this, Satan often lures people into immorality by playing on their basic needs." ("The Law of Chastity," *New Era,* January 1988, pp. 4–5.) . . .

Unfortunately, many parents, and thus their children, have trouble expressing love and affection. The problem seems to be more prevalent with fathers than with mothers, and older children seem to be more distant than younger. In a survey among high school students, only twenty-four percent said their fathers showed affection to them daily, while forty-nine percent said their mothers did. The problem is that too often this lack of affection is passed on to the next generation and an unfortunate cycle is perpetuated.

A friend of mine shared an excerpt from her grandfather's journal which illustrates the point. As a young man he had a strong desire to leave his native Norway and come to America. He recorded:

"In the fall of 1922, four other boys in the neighborhood and I decided to go to America. It took several months to get our papers ready.

"In January 1923, we were ready to leave home. On the morning I was to leave, my mother came upstairs at 4 A.M. to wake me up. As I lay there, she knelt by my bed and put her arm around me with her cheek against my cheek, and told me how she loved me and how she would miss me. She told me to be a good boy. She felt that she would not see me again in this life.

"I had been taught never to cry or show emotion, but at that moment I wanted to put my arms around her. Unfortunately, I let them lie still by my side under the covers. I didn't say or do anything, because I was a man. How could I be so soft to put my arms around my mother, or maybe cry and tell her how I loved her? I couldn't do that. It wasn't manly. How I have regretted that moment all these years!

"I got up, and she walked me two miles in the knee-deep snow to the bus stop. She helped me carry my suitcase. When I got on the bus, I shook hands with my mother and said good-bye. Now for fifty-two years I have regretted all this.

"Thirty-eight years after I came over to this country, I had a chance to go back to Norway for a visit. My mother had died eighteen years before. The first thing I did the first day I was there was to go to the graveyard. I didn't know where the graves were located. I searched up and down the rows till I finally came to the graves of my mother and father. I stood there and looked at them for a minute, and all my past days were going through my mind, especially the last day I saw my mother.

"I knelt down and put my arms around the marker. I put my cheek against her name, and those tears that I should have shed thirty-eight years earlier were shed there. I was not such a big man after all."

How unfortunate that this young man had been taught to "never cry or show emotion." I wonder who taught him that it wasn't manly to show emotion? Obviously it was not his mother. It's sad to imagine this young man with his arms around the tombstone expressing his love for his mother. We can learn a valuable lesson from this story. As parents, sons, and daughters, we need to learn how to convey love and affection among family members, or to continue if we have already been doing so. Such displays of affection can be a great protection in a day of sexual temptation. It is clear from research that youth who come from homes where love and affection are shown on a daily basis are much less willing to engage in immoral acts than those without such experiences. ("The Power of Love and Affection in our Families," in *Eternal Families,* Douglas E. Brinley, and Daniel K Judd, eds., Bookcraft: Salt Lake City, Utah, 1996, pp. 168–70.)

Please (1) hold family home evening every week; (2) make it a pleasant time to be together; (3) express love and appreciation for each member; and (4) reach out and touch other members of your family.

Another way to build relationships has to do with the amount of time we spend talking, reading, and sharing together as family members. Making mealtimes a time for dialogue between family members is helpful. One of the most important elements in winning the hearts of your children has to do with the amount of time you spend together as a family, or at least two of you, sharing ideas and feelings.

The primary aim of education is character. That should be one of our prime objectives as parents too.

President Ezra Taft Benson, counseled fathers: "Once you determine that a high priority in your life is to see that your wife and your children are happy, you will do all in your power to do so. I am not just speaking of satisfying material desires, but of filling other vital needs such as appreciation, compliments, comforting, encouraging, listening, and giving love and affection." (*Teachings,* p. 509.)

Principle #7: Individual and family prayer are the keys to retaining the Spirit of the Lord and keeping soft the hearts of each family member. Probably the most frequently given counsel to those who marry in the temple at the time of their ceremony is: "Tonight, before you two go to bed, would you kneel down and thank the Lord for each other, and make it a habit to do this every night from now on?" And yet, when you work with couples on a consistent basis, you find that none of them are praying together as a couple. My experience is that of Elder Joe J. Christensen who said:

Years ago, when it was common for a General Authority to tour a mission and interview all the missionaries, Elder Spencer W. Kimball, then a member of the Quorum of the Twelve, was visiting with an elder who was just about to finish his mission.

"When you get released, Elder, what are your plans?"

"Oh, I plan to go back to college," and with a smile added, "then I hope to fall in love and get married."

Elder Kimball shared this wise counsel, "Well, don't just pray to marry the one you love. *Instead, pray to love the one you marry.*"

We should pray to become more kind, courteous, humble, patient, forgiving, and *especially*, less selfish. . . .

And so the need to pray. Many church leaders and marriage counselors indicate that they have not seen one marriage in serious trouble where the couple was still praying together daily. When problems arise and marriages are threatened, praying together as a couple may be the most important remedy. (*Ensign*, May 1995, p. 64.)

How can you be angry and upset at someone you are praying for and praying with? If there is one principle that would save more marriages, it would be this one: Pray individually that you might become a better spouse and parent, pray together as a couple and ask the God of heaven to bless your home and family, and gather with your little ones and big ones together, and on your knees call down the powers of heaven on your little tribe. Prayer helps us develop Christlike character attributes.

Principle #8: Divorce is usually the worst answer to marital problems. President Harold B. Lee expressed his feelings about individuals who are giving up on their marriages too easily, and makes them a promise:

Sometimes, as we travel throughout the Church, a husband and wife will come to us and ask if, because they are not compatible in their marriage—they having had a temple marriage—it wouldn't be better if they were to free themselves from each other and then seek more congenial partners. To all such we say, whenever a couple who have been married in the temple say they are tiring of each other, it is an evidence that either one or both are not true to their temple covenants. Any couple married in the temple who are true to their covenants will grow dearer to each other, and love will find a deeper meaning on their golden wedding anniversary than on the day they were married in the house of the Lord. Don't you mistake that. (*Teachings of Harold B. Lee,* p. 249.)

And again his promise:

> Those who go to the marriage altar with love in their hearts, we might say to them in truth, if they will be true to the covenants that they take in the temple, fifty years after their marriage they can say to each another: "We must have not known what true love was when we were married, because we think so much more of each other today!" And so it will be if they will follow the counsel of their leaders and obey the holy, sacred instructions given in the temple ceremony; they will grow more perfectly in love even to a fulness of love in the presence of the Lord Himself. (*ibid.,* p. 243.)

Principle #9: Don't neglect sexual needs in your marriage, but keep that relationship within the bounds the Lord has set. President Spencer W. Kimball expressed these thoughts: "If you study divorces . . . you will find there are one, two, three, four reasons. Generally sex is the first. They did not get along sexually. They may not say that in the court. They may not even tell that to their attorneys, but that is the reason. . . . Husband and wife . . . are authorized, in fact they are commanded, to have proper sex when they are properly married for time and eternity. That does not mean that we need to go to great extremes. That does not mean that a woman is the servant of her husband. It does not mean that any man has a right to demand sex anytime that he might want it. He should be reasonable and understanding and it should be a general program between the two, so they understand and everybody is happy about it." (Edward L. Kimball, ed., *The Teachings of Spencer W. Kimball,* p. 312.)

Sexual intimacy is a powerful expression of marital love in physical, emotional, and caring ways. When a marriage prospers in the non-sexual areas of the marriage, sexual intimacy becomes a natural expression of love that already exists. Just as sexual relations can strengthen a marriage, so does a great marriage increase interest in and a desire to give of oneself to a caring spouse in ways that meet the needs of both partners.

"Sexual union is lawful in wedlock, and if participated in with right intent is honorable and sanctifying," said President Joseph F. Smith (*Gospel Doctrine,* p. 309). Keep intimate relationship in good condition with intimate encounters that allow you to express your love and devotion to each other in a way that transcends our usual daily exchanges. Wives should remember that sexual relations are therapeutic to husbands, and men tend to equate love and sex. Men must remember that wives are more interested in intimate exchanges when they are treated as a wife ought to be treated by a righteous husband. A good husband and father are good places to begin to improve the sexual union of two marrieds; a husband who is sensitive and kind to the feelings of his wife, and who pitches in to do his part to help with the housework and parenting.

Principle #10: Relationships must be monitored continually. I have heard a parent say, "I don't know why Church members are having such a hard time rearing their children. My son (or daughter) is only twelve but he (she) bears testimony almost every fast Sunday." Wise parents have learned that much can happen between ages 12 and 15; between 14 and 17; between 16 and 19. Relationships can be quite fragile if we are not attentive to them. An episode of anger by a father or mother can destroy weeks and months of "good" behavior with children.

In your family, who takes responsibility to correct ill-feelings, sins, or mistakes? Allowing bad feelings to exist between members of the same family, to allow them to go on and on, where one spouse uses the silent treatment in an effort to hurt or punish the other spouse, where one simply is unwilling to discuss family matters is not only frustrating to each other but such behavior is contrary to good sense and the spirit of the gospel of

Jesus Christ. It was the Lord who commanded, "whosoever is angry with his brother [spouse, child] shall be in danger of his judgment. . . . First be reconciled to thy [spouse, child] brother, and then come unto me with full purpose of heart, and I will receive you." (3 Nephi 12:22, 24.)

Adam found himself in a difficult situation after Eve had partaken of the fruit in the garden. She would now be forced to leave the garden for disobeying a law that had a serious consequence—death. Adam considered the situation, realized that this was his wife, his eternal companion, and decided to join her. He gave up his life for his wife. He could have refused to go with her. He could have chosen to remain alone in the garden. But that would have negated the great commandment to "multiply and replenish the earth." He loved his wife and was willing to walk with her through the trials that they would so quickly face. (Going through childbirth could have been enough to make Eve change her mind had she known!) But this first couple were willing to walk the path together, arm-in-arm, and face whatever life presented them.

Is it not the same today, tomorrow, and forever with every couple? Do we not make the same commitments to each other at marriage? Do we not promise God that we will both give ourselves and receive each other in an eternal covenant? We realize that we have both strengths and weaknesses that will become more obvious as time passes. Before marriage our strengths and potential look so promising while we minimize any weaknesses we see. But marriage has the power of "Miracle-Grow" in making weaknesses blossom, while if we are not careful we end up using the "Round-Up" of sarcasm and criticism to kill strengths. Together we are raising the most important crop of all—youngsters fresh from the presence of God who have been assigned to come at this time in the world's history.

Divorce may be necessary in rare cases to preserve the sanity and emotional health of a husband or wife when there is no repentance on the part of a spouse. Surely God is displeased when a couple leaves their [His] children to founder on the reefs of broken covenants and promises, to say nothing of the impact that divorce may have on the children's outlook in future years. Fathering is a skill we imitate. Good fathering comes from watching a good father. The same is true of mothering. These divine attributes are passed from parent to child.

Another observation: Divorce never ends. In spite of the parents' separation, children go on living their lives and the need for two parents is still evident. As the children grow, both parents are still involved in their lives as to schooling and health expenses, wedding receptions, and grandchildren. No wonder the Lord made it clear that covenant people do not divorce unless serious sins are involved.

Counseling is often an admission that we are not sufficiently humble to resolve our own disagreements. Obtaining advice, listening to new ideas, are always a necessary part of our growth. But too often people go to counseling looking for a "referee," one who will tell the spouse how wrong he or she is.

A strong marriage comes from living gospel principles. Let me give an analogy. Suppose a dear friend came to you and said: "I have gone inactive. The Church just doesn't mean to me what it once did. I just don't think it has all the answers." What would you do in such a situation? Would you say: "Well, that's too bad. I guess that's just the way life is sometimes. What works for one may not work for another." No, of course not, because you know that the person has stopped living the laws that build strong testimonies. You would not give him up; you would plead with him to get back to the scriptures, back to personal prayer, back to the things that brought him into the Church or activity in the first place.

The same holds true for marriage. How do you "fall out of love"? It is a matter of covenant breaking, of apathy, of a failure to nourish the relationship, taking too much for granted, little sharing of heart and soul, a loss of intimacy. It is possible for a great love to shrink; it is also possible for a new love to grow into an avalanche of passion and gratitude.

To keep our love alive we must "feed it" regularly. Love is based upon the self-revelations of one soul to another and upon mutual sharing and service; in meeting each other's needs in the routine of daily living. It comes from sharing marital intimacy in a relationship of trust where expressing love is free and unhindered and unembarrassed. Money management, interfering in-laws, apartment living-space, children, housekeeping, recreation or use of leisure time, and a host of other events and actions confront us in the course of sharing our lives and love. The steps that lead to a strong marital love include being therapeutic to each other in resolving problems and daily challenges, being reminded of eternal covenants, and lifting each other to higher levels of commitment and love.

Any person who would like to improve his marriage must give the required time to the relationship. A relationship needs a fair amount of attention to keep it working smoothly. By nourishing the relationship each day, we are better prepared for any eventuality.

To keep the love light burning there must be a conformity to healthy principles of relationships, increased application of Christlike principles—charity, patience, meekness, forgiveness, overlooking trivial matters, long-suffering, turning the other cheek, frequent communication, mutual sacrifice for the welfare of the spouse, and an intimate trust in each other's fidelity. Marital love is a source of contentment, of peace, of calm assurance of being loved, of a desire to do all within one's power to keep the marital ship on course, and sharing the adventure together as we sail across seas that vary from peaceful quiet to storms that can challenge the voyage.

How Does Marital Love Die?

Because marriage has life, it is subject to weaknesses and even death. We have all seen it—in the form of divorce that the prophets have labeled a modern scourge. Observe the life of any divorcee. Since marital love is a fruit of the Spirit, it is possible to watch marital love shrink as one's spirituality shrinks. This comes about when we take each other for granted, when interest in each other wanes. Covenants are ignored. Fatigue, boredom, or a lack of interchange can have harmful effects.

Differences in solutions to common problems may develop into power struggles where being "right" is more important than preserving the peace. These can often increase to such magnitude that they endanger the relationship.

Most often, however, the loss of marital love is due to finding fault with each other, that is, in the actions and attitudes of the spouse. This fault-finding springs into existence through the misinterpretation of minor actions on the part of the spouse. Soon every action of the partner seems wrong and seems to poison other areas of the marriage that have been such a source of pleasure and mutual good feelings in the past. Their vision distorts their view of marriage, and feelings are quick to subside.

The death of marital love is easily seen as normal pleasantries, the sharing of ideas and feelings, and intimate contact begin to dry up. Escape mechanisms—TV, sports, movies, gardening—replace togetherness; the cold hand of selfishness replaces the former admiration and willingness to do all for one's spouse. Soon love is drained, and two partners look at each other with glazed eyes, wondering how their relationship could have been destroyed as if by termites, a nibble at a time, who ate away the seemingly formidable structure which seemed so indestructible at one time. Like the mighty oak, they will fall if there is not an immediate treatment by ripping away the rotten lumber.

However, there is always something of that first marriage that is never lost even in subsequent marriages. There is a feeling that something has been forfeited; that one did not give his or her best. In the quiet moments of one's inner life, there is a hollowness, a regret for allowing something of value to be destroyed. Once lost, it is difficult to retrieve. Once gone, it is nigh impossible to restore. Once a possession of some value has disappeared, there is little to replace it. Freedom is lost. Temper is sharp. Defensiveness is the rule of the day. No one will take responsibility. The tongue continues its criticism. And most critical to the process, God is disappointed while Satan laughs gleefully. Such is the nature of many souls whose marital ship has been wrecked on the shoals of telestial navigation, insufficient mapping, and poor maintenance of the helm that has rusted on its hinges. Two souls, who started out on the trip of their life, have now lost their way on a sea of destruction.

SUMMARY AND CONCLUSIONS

We have the opportunity and responsibility to model correct principles of stable marriages and happy children. In one generation we can lift families to a new level of satisfaction and functioning if we remind ourselves frequently of the part marriage and family life play in the eternal framework of God's plan. We must give families our highest priority.

Mental health is greatly affected by our understanding of our origin as sons and daughters of God and living true to that destiny. Good mental health begins with individuals whose marriages bring out the best in them and who will then rear their children to accept the values taught them by parents who place marriage and family in their proper perspective. We can produce healthy individuals. It is not a mystery. Here is the simple formula once more: *stable marriages produce stable children who produce stable adults who create stable marriages.* Here is what the results sound like:

> I am so thankful for parents who taught me the standards I needed to have and then taught me how to keep those standards high. I am grateful that my parents were my best friends, because I've had so many friends that sacrificed their standards and rebelled against their parents. I never understood how parents and their children couldn't get along, because I talked to my parents all of the time. I told them everything and as a result their trust in me grew. I still couldn't do things that they thought would place me in a bad environment and I still always had to tell them where I was going and when I would be back, but I was given more freedom and with that freedom more responsibility. One activity in our family that I really appreciated was family prayer. Every morning we would gather in the front room where we would read the scriptures and then kneel in family prayer. Immediately following the prayer we had a family hug. What a way to start the day! There was a manifestation of

both our Heavenly Father's love and our earthly parents love. I attribute my success and strength to my family and the love that was shown to me throughout my growing up years.

We will all have to answer some day as to how well we did in these stewardships of family. Following is a statement President David O. McKay made to a group of Church employees in 1965.

Let me assure you, Brethren, that some day you will have a personal priesthood interview with the Savior himself. If you are interested, I will tell you the order in which he will ask you to account for your earthly responsibilities.

First, He will request an accountability report about your relationship with your wife. Have you actively been engaged in making her happy and ensuring that her needs have been met as an individual?

Second, He will want an accountability report about each of your children individually. He will . . . request information about your relationship to each and every child.

Third, He will want to know what you personally have done with the talents you were given in the [premortal life].

Fourth, He will want a summary of your activity in your Church assignments. He will not necessarily be interested in what assignments you have had, for in his eyes the home teacher and a mission president are probably equals, but he will request a summary of how you have been of service to your fellow man in your Church assignments.

Fifth, He will have no interest in how you earned your living, but if you were honest in all your dealings.

Sixth, He will ask for an accountability on what you have done to contribute in a positive manner to your community, state, country, and the world." (In Stephen R. Covey, *The Divine Center*, Bookcraft, 1982, pp. 54–55.)

Gospel doctrines and the atonement of Jesus Christ are directed to save the family unit. We live in the final dispensation prior to the coming of the Lord to usher in the great Millennial era. We must have a Zion people prepared for that great thousand year work when we get all the mistakes of the first six thousand years corrected; when all those worthy of being sealed together in marriage and family units will be completed. The future is exciting. What a time in which to live. As Latter-day Saints we have a window of opportunity before war reaches out its ugly hand to take our young men back into the wars that will precede the Second Coming.

Every worthy young man *can* serve a mission. Missions will humble a prosperous generation of young men so that they will be worthy of the great privilege to marry and rear their children in righteousness. We are a temple-building people. The Church has an international presence since more than half of the Saints live out of the United States. We are prospering. Our young people are becoming educated and can not only compete with the best, but lead the way. The media is looking favorably on the Church. The President of the Church has met with the President of the United States about a Proclamation on the Family. The snowball (or stone cut without hands) is rolling forth.

We must not be careless with the great trust we have been given. What happens in our homes holds the key to the future of this last great effort.

What else could the Lord do for us that he hasn't already done? We have the standard works in one binding, clean and comfortable Church buildings financed from headquarters rather than the local Saints having to raise the funds; family history centers; missionary training centers to prepare missionaries both in languages and proselyting principles to teach and testify; and stakes are being established worldwide. Now is our time. Now is our day.

Let us be valiant in our service to our God. It is his work. We have prospered now for decades. We have the means to be his people. We need to re-double our efforts with inactive Saints, some of whom are very good at being inactive. Let's not let any new convert become inactive or leave the kingdom. Let's get our young people mission-prepared and temple-bound. Ephraim and Manasseh, it is our task. Are we ready?

Our families are the key to the bright future ahead of us.

Notes

1. Melchizedek's people were translated to heaven and the city "sought for Enoch" (see Joseph Smith Translation [JST] Genesis 14:25–40). Apparently the people of Jethro were righteous, but we have no indication that this group was large.

2. Even apart from their lack of priesthood authority, offshoots and apostate groups would be incapable of carrying out this latter-day mission. A worldwide missionary effort, gathering records for the dead, and building temples can only be done by a church of sufficient size and strength. Even with a Church of ten to twenty million people, the task will be formidable.

3. See D&C 101:40–41.

4. I can hear someone reading this saying, "You don't know my husband (wife). If I don't respond, they continue to be nasty, or they will not let me walk away. They will grab me and force me to stay and listen to their complaints." If that is true in your particular case, you need help from priesthood leaders who understand what is going on in your home.

5. See Brett's article in *Eternal Companions,* Bookcraft, 1995, chapter 10, "True Doctrine as Marital Therapy," pp. 151–76.

6. All spirit is matter (D&C 131:7–8). Therefore, spirit bodies are matter, but are more refined matter than can be seen with mortal, telestial eyes. However, spirits can see each other, can touch one another. They have bodies of celestial matter with spirit in their veins; hence they are spirit children.

7. These five concepts are modified from Bruce R. McConkie's

Doctrinal New Testament Commentary, (Bookcraft), vol. 1, pp. 546–49, 604–8.

8. Individual psychotic problems may develop when individuals sin and fall short of the high ideals born of the doctrinal principle that we are the children of God with the potential to become like him—exaltation. Through Christ's atonement and resurrection, and repentance on our part, we may attain eternal life on conditions of obedience to gospel principles. In contrast, it is possible for people to become frustrated or rebel against high ideals when they fail to discipline themselves to live by the required standards.

9. Or we could say "on this earth." Many who die before marriage, or who have kept their baptismal and temple covenants but who did not marry, or were married to individuals who did not honor covenants and commandments, will find partners in the spirit world or following the resurrection, but it will be here on this earth that such choices are made. After we are assigned to degrees of glory as resurrected personages, there is "no more marriage or giving in marriage."

10. Hopefully re-marriage will allow couples to get back on the path to eternal life. This is not to say that both parties are equally guilty at the time of divorce, but I've seen few friendly divorces; usually bitterness and rancor are associated with the dissolution of marriage, and less than celestial attitudes.

11. There are limits, of course, to what is tolerated even in an immoral society. Hurting children in any physical or emotional way; battering women and children, is wrong. But somehow abortion is solely the woman's decision up to the time of birth.

12. Randall A. Wright, see *Protecting Your Family in an X-Rated World,* Salt Lake City: Deseret Book, 1988.

13. Resurrected celestialized beings can create spirit children because they have spirit in their veins, not blood; thus their children are called spirit children. Yet, all spirit is matter (see D&C 131:7–8).

14. For references on Heavenly Mother, see J. Reuben Clark, CR, 1951:57; Spencer W. Kimball, *Ensign,* May 1978, p. 6; Neal A. Maxwell, *Ensign,* May, 1978:11.

15. It is the role of the priesthood to protect and honor women. Men are to be prepared to give their lives to protect and bless their sweethearts. Wisely our Heavenly Father has not told us much about our heavenly mother. From here on I will only refer to Heavenly Father, but it is understood that we have two heavenly parents.

16. God is God not because he does not know what evil is; he knows better than anyone else. But he chooses to live only by principles that lead to happiness for himself and others.

17. See my chapter entitled, "Not Without Hope: Singles and Those 'Unequally Yoked,'" in *Strengthening Your Marriage and Family,* Bookcraft, 1994, pp. 77–96.

18. Spirits are unable to procreate other spirits; otherwise Satan would be able to raise up spirits who would follow him.

19. The Father's children are adults before this earth life, and we will be adults after death. When we speak of eternal families, we mean married couples will have access to each other in the celestial kingdom because we live on the same planet and continue our family connections. Of course, little children who die in mortality will be resurrected as they were laid down, then will grow to the full stature of their spirits following the resurrection.

20. See chapter 10, "Eternal Families—A Unique Doctrine," in the author's earlier book *Strengthening Your Marriage and Family,* Bookcraft, 1994.

21. Christian theology as taught in the world allows that men and women will live again, but not in the married state.

22. The term "love of God" may mean either a love "for" God, or God's love for us. Either way, it seems to connote a mutual appreciation and love for each other.

23. Of course we are saved by grace, but works are an indication that we accept the Savior's atonement, and our works will influence our final judgment.

24. See D&C 132:17; 131:1–4.

Index

on gospel living, 3, 48
on love, 89
on marital realities, 58
on missionary service,
118–19
on parental accountability,
14
on physical intimacy, 128
on prayer, 127
on preserving families, 10
on scripture study, 61–62
on selfishness, 89, 103
on success, 48
on working mothers, 120

— L —

last days
Brigham Young on, 10
Lee, Harold B.
on divorce, 127–28
on eternal marriage, 128
on exaltation, 45–46
on gospel living, 10
on love, 128
on missionary work, 10
on success, 48
Lehi
as an example for us, 72
as a prototype of Christ, 68
response to Sariah's con-
cerns, 68–70, 72
love
expressing, 123–26
Ezra Taft Benson on parents
showing, 80

Harold B. Lee on, 128
how marital love dies,
132–34
Howard W. Hunter on par-
ents showing, 74
and immorality, 124
importance of nurturing
marital love, 131–32
importance of parents modeling, 74, 76, 80–81
Spencer W. Kimball on, 89
touching, as an expression
of, 123–24
"love of God," 63, 65

— M —

marital conflict
example of Lehi and Sariah
resolving, 65–72
few scriptural examples of, 65
marriage, civil
logical deductions from,
39–40
for time only, 25
marriage, eternal
applying gospel principles to
improve, 61–65
and the Atonement, 25
Bruce R. McConkie on, 51
cancellation of sealing, 26
central focus of plan of salvation, 25, 32–34
changes our perspective, 73
children greatest source of
happiness in, 122

Pratt, Orson, on Satan,
    29–30
prayer
    as a couple, 126–27
    Joe J. Christensen on, 127
    Spencer W. Kimball on, 127
premortal life
    Brigham Young on, 22–23
    First Presidency message on,
        21–22
    Proclamation on the Family
        on, 22, 49
    progress limited in, 23
pride
    as a cause of divorce, 90
    difficulty of admitting,
        102–3
    examples of husbands',
        107–10
    examples of wives', 110–11
    Ezra Taft Benson on, 89
    fighting, in our homes, 115
    indicators of pride, 103–7
    indicators of softened hearts,
        112–14
    taking offense, 114–15
Proclamation on the Family
    text of, 48–50
    See also First Presidency mes-
        sages
procreation, Proclamation on
    the Family on, 49
prosperity
    as an aid in preparing for the
        second coming, 2
    as a cause of spiritual com-
        placency, 1–2, 9

— R —

rationalizing, 42, 92
relationships, family, 129–30
repentance
    accepting responsibility for
        changing behavior, 92–95
    difficulties of, 90–91
    F. Burton Howard on, 95
    healing power of, 95–101
    offering apologies, 91, 95–100
    power of the Atonement ac-
        cessed through, 100
    rationalizing behavior, 92
    recognizing wrongdoing, 95
restoration of the gospel,
    progress since, 7–8
resurrection
    behavior changed by under-
        standing of, 63–65
    ramifications of, 34–35
road rage, 93

— S —

Sariah
    character of, 71–72
    comforted by Lehi's re-
        sponse to concerns, 70
    complains to Lehi, 65–68
Satan
    desires to destroy marriages,
        30
    Orson Pratt on, 29–30
    unable to marry, 29–30,
        38–39
    unable to procreate, 55